Stories fro[m]

BY

R. M. OGILVIE

OXFORD UNIVERSITY PRESS

Oxford University Press, Walton Street, Oxford OX2 6DP
OXFORD LONDON GLASGOW
NEW YORK TORONTO MELBOURNE AUCKLAND
KUALA LUMPUR SINGAPORE HONG KONG TOKYO
DELHI BOMBAY CALCUTTA MADRAS KARACHI
NAIROBI DAR ES SALAAM CAPE TOWN

AND ASSOCIATED COMPANIES IN
BEIRUT BERLIN IBADAN MEXICO CITY NICOSIA

Oxford is a trade mark of Oxford University Press

Text © Oxford University Press 1970

Original drawings and maps © Alan Sorrell 1970

First published 1973
Reprinted 1980, 1984

PHOTOSET BY BAS PRINTERS LTD., WALLOP, HAMPSHIRE AND
PRINTED IN HONG KONG

Contents

	page
Stories from Livy	1
Romulus and Remus	6
Hercules and Cacus	9
The Rape of the Sabine Women	11
Two Women	22
The Fall of Gabii	28
The Expulsion of the Tarquins	30
Horatius Cocles	34
The Story of Coriolanus	38
Cremera	41
Cincinnatus	44
Verginia	46
Sp. Maelius	48
The Fall of Veii	51
The Faliscan School-master	57
The Capture of Rome	59
The Fall of Manlius	63
The Son of Manlius Torquatus	69
The Caudine Forks	72
The Death of P. Decius	79
Crossing the Alps	82
Lake Trasimene	89
Scipio and Allucius	94
The Story of Sophonisba	98
The Siege of Syracuse	100
A Mutiny	104
The Battle of Metaurus	109
Perseus and Demetrius	113
The Death of Hannibal	119
Index	121

List of Photographs

The Emperor Augustus, *sculpture from Museo delle Terme, Rome*	facing page 1
The Roman Forum today	page 3
An Etruscan cinerary urn in the shape of a house	5
The Capitoline wolf, *sculpture from Museo nuovo del Campidoglio, Rome*	6
Hercules, *sculpture from Museo nuovo del Campidoglio, Rome*	9
The Tarpeian rock today	14
Metrius Curtius, *relief from Museo Mussolini, Rome*	15
Horatius and the bridge, *coin from Bibliotheque Nationale, Paris*	35
The walls of Veii today	51
Lake Albano today	53
An underground tunnel at Veii	54
Apollo, *terracotta from Museo Nazionale di Villa Giulia, Rome*	56
A Gallic Warrior, *statuette from Deutsches Archaeologisches Institut, Rome*	67
A Samnite Warrior, *bronze from the Louvre, Paris*	72
An Alpine pass	86
Lake Trasimene	90

List of Maps

Plan of Rome	page 21
The surroundings of Rome and Corioli	39
Veii	42
Samnium and the Caudine Forks	75
Hannibal's route	83
The Mediterranean	101
Spain	106

Acknowledgements

We should like to thank the following for permission to reproduce photographs:
> Aerofilms Ltd., p. 86;
> Bibliotheque Nationale, Paris, p. 33;
> Deutsches Archäologisches Institut, Rome, pp. 67, 72;
> Fototeca Unione, pr Accademia Americana, Rome, pp. 3, 14;
> The Mansell Collection, frontispiece and pp. 5, 6, 9, 15, 51, 54, 56.

Augustus

Stories from Livy

Two thousand years ago, Italy was the greatest power in the world and Rome, its capital, was the largest and finest city that had ever been built. One can only imagine its size and wealth by comparing it with the British Empire and London in the nineteenth century or with the United States and New York today. The Romans had conquered all Europe, North Africa and the Middle East. For 400 years Britain was a province in the Roman Empire, ruled by a governor who was sent out every few years from Rome, policed by the Roman army and administered by Roman laws. The British came to live like Romans, in cities instead of in scattered huts, speaking Latin rather than Celtic. And it was because Britain was a Roman province that missionaries such as St. Patrick and St. Columba brought Christianity to this country. But when the Roman army left Britain in A.D. 410 and the Roman Empire broke up in the face of invasions from Germany and Russia, Roman civilization continued in a different form in monasteries and at the courts of kings like King Arthur and King Alfred.

So our history owes a lot to Rome and it is worth finding out what kind of people the Romans were and what sort of a place Rome was. For Rome had not always been large and powerful. It began as a small village of shepherds. The Romans were just as impressed as we are at the process by which it grew into a great city and they preserved many stories about the most exciting episodes in their past. But for a long time life at Rome was too unsettled and violent for anyone to collect these stories into a real history of Rome. From 130–30 B.C. there was a series of civil wars and riots and disturbances as different ambitious politicians—Marius and Sulla, Caesar and Pompey—quarrelled and fought. People looked back to the old days and felt that civilization was in the melting-pot. Even Cicero, one of the greatest speakers and writers of the time, said that Rome's days were numbered. Then confidence returned when Augustus emerged after 31 B.C. as undisputed ruler of Rome and restored peace and stability to the Roman empire.

This new atmosphere of hope and pride encouraged many writers to look back on the obstacles which Rome had overcome. Because they believed that they were entering on a new age of lasting prosperity, they wanted to trace the stages of that progress. Horace in his *Odes* and Vergil in his epic, the *Aeneid*, both stress the connection between Rome's past achievements and her present success. To illustrate these points they go back to the familiar legends of Roman heroes—Aeneas, Romulus, Cincinnatus, Camillus, and so on. So it was natural that someone should undertake the task of compiling a history which would show how the character and deeds of earlier Romans had enabled Rome to triumph over difficulties and reach the top. The man who did this was Livy (Titus Livius, as he was called) who was born about 65 B.C. in Padua, a thriving commercial town in the north of Italy. Livy seems to have come from a typical provincial middle-class family—the sort of family which had suffered worst from the disturbances of the preceding two or three generations and which stood to gain most from peace. He was given a good education, which in those days meant chiefly the study of Greek and Roman poetry and philosophy and the art of public speaking. But although he looked to Rome as the centre of the world and took the first opportunity of making his home there, he did not try to make a public career for himself. Instead he decided to devote his life to writing the history of Rome from its foundation down to his own day. It was a task that was to occupy the rest of his life from about 28 B.C. to his death in A.D. 17 and which filled 145 volumes (35 of them still survive). Livy was obviously well enough off to be able to live a life of study and retirement but his ability also soon attracted the attention of Augustus who was eager to help and encourage the young historian. We do not know how close an eye Augustus kept on the progress of the work, except that he persuaded Livy to alter one story and appointed him literary adviser to his great-nephew, the future Emperor Claudius.

The first sight of Rome, with its wide colonnades and marble buildings, must have thrilled Livy—as it still thrills every visitor on arrival—and his admiration will have been all the greater because he was a provincial and not a native of Rome. It is remarkable how almost all the great writers of the time—Horace, Vergil, Ovid, Propertius—came from the provinces and were therefore inspired by the magnificence of Rome in comparison with their own humble

The Roman forum today

backgrounds. But at the same time Livy brought a strong commonsense and a streak of puritanism from his home town which saved him from being corrupted by the free and easy life of the capital. Padua was a very moral, straight-laced place whereas Roman society was easy-going. These qualities helped Livy to imagine what life must have been like in the old, strict days and to picture the sort of grim Romans who had put patriotism before everything else.

Livy's chief interest, therefore, was to make the past live. He wanted his readers to appreciate how their ancestors behaved, how they talked and how they thought. This was much more important to him than to find out precisely when a particular battle was fought or whether there were 2,000 or 20,000 Carthaginian casualties.

3

By our standards Livy's approach to history seems careless and inaccurate but his interests were quite different from those of a modern historian. He was much less interested in discovering what really happened than in re-creating the character and feelings of the people who were involved. We should think of him as a historical novelist rather than as a historian, setting out to write a dramatic story even if this involved taking liberties with the actual facts. But he differed from a historical novelist such as John Buchan or Mary Renault in that he did not just want to make up a good yarn. He had a serious purpose as well. He really did believe that the Romans of old were braver, finer and better than in his day and that if he could inspire his readers to imitate them they would be able to bring back the glories of the past. It is after all true that the welfare of a country depends upon the determination and ambition of its citizens.

So Livy collected the old stories and retold them in his own way. You will find that he always emphasizes the good qualities of the Romans. Camillus' respect for the gods is responsible for his final victory over the Veii and the Gauls. His humanity is strikingly illustrated by the tale about the Faliscan schoolmaster. 'Poor but honest' is the lesson of Cincinnatus whereas the evils of money and power are brought out in the life of Tarquin. It is the same all the way through; every story points a moral. This could easily degenerate into a series of boring sermons but Livy avoids that by his skill in the actual telling. Each incident is dramatized so that the reader can really see and hear it happening for himself. The key to this lies in the way in which Livy makes clear what the main actors are thinking and feeling. We sympathize with Coriolanus' doubts when he meets his mother; we share Romulus's pride in his newly founded city; we can feel the hopes and fears which filled Hannibal's army as it struggled over the Alps. All this makes history live. And Livy added something else. Instead of just telling us what people did or even what they felt, he made them speak. The climax of almost every story is a short speech or dialogue between the main characters. Livy is not afraid to use the sort of language which he thinks that they might really have used, so that you get an impression of an authentic conversation.

This was something new in Roman history and it was never to be repeated. Livy's History became a classic, which was often copied and often abridged but never rivalled. And since our knowledge of the history of early Rome depends very largely on him, his words should be left to tell their own story.

To a modern reader there may seem to be too many battles and sudden deaths for his taste. Livy disliked violence no less than we do, but war did occupy as great a place in Roman life as it does in our own and nothing is gained by turning a blind eye on such facts or pretending that they do not exist. Livy accepts war but does not glorify it. Rather, he recognizes that in war men often perform exceptional acts of heroism and of humanity, when their characters are put to the most severe test. These acts do not in any way justify war but they should never be belittled. Rome had won her position in the world partly by diplomacy, partly by chance but chiefly by dogged perseverance in battle. These wars, therefore, should be remembered because they were the occasion of the rise of Rome and because they often showed the ancient Romans, whether in defeat or victory, at their best.

The Romans believed that the earliest inhabitants of Rome were shepherds who built huts on the Palatine Hill about 750 B.C. This belief was proved to be true when archaeologists found the remains of such huts there and were able to date them to between 800 and 700 B.C. Although only the foundations of the huts remained, we are able to tell what they looked like because these early shepherds buried the ashes of their dead in model huts made of clay and many of these, like the one in the picture, have been found. It was in a hut like this Faustulus sheltered Romulus and Remus according to the story which Livy tells.

A hut urn

Romulus and Remus

The Capitoline Wolf

The story that Romulus and Remus were exposed, like Moses, in a basket and looked after by a wolf was very popular at Rome. At an early date the Romans erected a statue of the wolf to commemorate it.

There was a king named Proca who ruled over a rich country, called Alba Longa. When Proca died he left his kingdom to his elder son Numitor, but Amulius, the younger son, drove his brother out. He killed Numitor's sons and made his daughter Rhea a Vestal Virgin. He pretended that this was an honour for her but it was really to prevent her having children who might challenge him.

Fate spoiled his plan because Rhea did after all have children; twin boys. She claimed that Mars, the god of war, was their father but this claim did not help her, for the king put her in prison and ordered the babies to be drowned in the Tiber. The men took the babies in a basket down to the river and put it in the water. But the Tiber was flooded and instead of flinging the basket into the middle they had left it in a rather stagnant backwater. So when the floods subsided a bit the basket was left high and dry. The story goes that a she-wolf came down from the hills to this deserted stretch of river for a drink and hearing the hungry babies cry went to investigate the basket. When a man called Faustulus, the king's shepherd, came on the scene he found the wolf gently licking the babies and giving them milk. This man took the children back with him to his hut and gave them to his wife Larentia to look after, who called them Romulus and Remus.

The boys lived there helping the shepherd in his work until they were fifteen or so. When they had finished their work in the farm they would go off into the mountains to hunt. They became so tough and fearless that they attacked not only wild beasts but even robbers. The robbers however were furious when Romulus and Remus outwitted them. They waited their chance, and one day they laid an ambush for them. Romulus managed to fight his way out but Remus was captured. The robbers took him to the king Amulius and accused him of making raids on Numitor's land. So Remus was handed over to Numitor to be punished.

Now Faustulus had been pretty sure right from the beginning that the twins were princes of royal blood. He knew that two boys had been exposed by the king's orders at just about the time that he had found the babies, but he didn't want to tell anyone until he had to. When Remus was captured Faustulus was so frightened that he told Romulus the whole story.

Romulus didn't call his gang together for he didn't feel strong enough to challenge the king openly; but he arranged for his friends the shepherds to make their way to the palace. They were to come in twos and threes by different routes and to meet him at an agreed time. Numitor, who already suspected that Remus was his grandson from his princely behaviour, also let him go to Alba Longa with a large body of men to help his brother. So Romulus and Remus joined forces and killed Amulius.

Numitor then called a council at which he revealed everything that had happened, how he had been maltreated by Amulius, how Romulus and Remus were his grandsons who had been thrown into the Tiber, and how they had been rescued, brought up by a shepherd and eventually recognized. Romulus and Remus replied by hailing their grandfather as the true king and a storm of cheers and applause greeted their words.

Now that Numitor was safely king of Alba, Romulus and Remus decided to go and found a city of their own near where they had been brought up. There were plenty of people keen to come and live in their city and everything would have gone well if Romulus and Remus had not been so ambitious. Since they were twins and the right to the throne could not be decided simply by age, they agreed to leave it to the gods. Remus was the first to receive a sign from heaven. But scarcely had six vultures flown over the Aventine Hill where he was living, than 12 vultures appeared to Romulus on the Palatine Hill. Each was saluted king by his followers, Remus because he got the message first from the gods, Romulus because his was twice as strong. Remus was so confident that he rashly taunted his brother by jumping over the wall which he was building. In a fury Romulus killed him saying 'So perish all who cross my walls'. In this way Romulus became king and the city was called Rome after him.

Hercules and Cacus

Another popular legend tells why Hercules was worshipped as a god from the very beginning of the city at a spot close to the Palatine Hill which came to be known as the Great Circus and where chariot-races and games were held.

Romulus began his reign by fortifying the Palatine where he had lived as a child, and he set up altars to the gods as all the Albans did. But in particular he worshipped a Greek god, Hercules, and this is why.

Once upon a time Hercules slew a giant called Geryones. He then collected all Geryones' cattle, which were an exceptionally beautiful lot, and drove them across the Tiber, swimming after them himself. On the other side he found a lush green pasture where the cattle could rest and feed. After a good dinner, tired by the strenuous journey, he lay down and went to sleep. While he slept, a man called Cacus, who was a shepherd but who also practised burglary on the side, came up to see who was camping near his cave. He was so impressed by the beauty of Hercules' herd that he decided to steal it to add to his own. If he had just driven the cows into his cave their footmarks would have shown which way they had

Hercules

gone. So he picked out the best of the herd and dragged them backwards by the tail into his hiding-place. In the morning, when Hercules woke up, he saw at once that some of his cattle were missing. But when he went to the cave nearby looking for footprints, he discovered that all the prints led the wrong way—from the cave to the field where he had slept. He was quite bewildered. He decided that he had better get away from that enchanted place as fast as he could with the remains of his herd. But as he began to go some of the cows mooed, missing their companions, and immediately the stolen cows answered from the cave. Hercules rushed back to the spot. Cacus tried to oppose him and called for help from his fellow shepherds, but Hercules felled him with his club. The shepherds quickly ran up and surrounded Hercules, accusing him of murder and claiming that they had caught him red-handed. Hercules was saved by the timely arrival of the king, Evander, who did not have much official power but was respected partly because he had invented the alphabet and partly because his mother was said to be a goddess. When Evander asked what had happened, Hercules told him the whole story. Seeing at once that Hercules was both larger and stronger than an ordinary man, Evander asked his name, and on hearing it, he said, 'Welcome, Hercules! My mother, who was inspired from Heaven, told me that one day you would become a god. She foretold that a great altar would be built to you here and that the most powerful nation in the world would worship you at it'. Hercules took his hand and said he would fulfil the prophecy by building an altar there and then. The shepherds chose the most splendid beast from the herd and for the first time made sacrifice to Hercules. And this custom has lasted down to the present day.

The Rape of the Sabine Women

There was another little village on a neighbouring hill called the Esquiline. This village was inhabited by people called Sabines who had come down from the hills of central Italy and settled near Rome. The two villages decided that it would be more sensible to join together and form a single community. The Romans, however, pictured this union as a much more exciting event and Livy tells how Romulus engineered the abduction of a large number of Sabine women in order to make a large city that included both the Palatine and the Esquiline.

Rome was by now strong enough to take on all comers, but it was a town of men·only and since there were no women there could be no children. The men would grow old and die, and if something were not done about it there would be no one to take their place. So Romulus decided to consult his Senate, a body of 100 chief men in the state. On their advice he sent ambassadors to the states round about asking them to become allies of Rome and to allow Roman men to marry their women. Everything, he argued, had to start from small beginnings, and it was the same with cities. If they worked hard, and enjoyed good luck, they would in no time be famous and powerful. For he was certain they had heaven's favour and that the other states would one day be proud to have helped them. Everyone was much too frightened of the great city growing up at Rome to listen to these arguments, and so they sent the ambassadors away without answer. The Romans were so angry that war was inevitable. But Romulus was anxious to fight on ground of his own choosing, so as to give the Romans the best chance of winning. This was his plan. He arranged a great festival (in honour of Neptune) and advertised it everywhere. The Romans made tremendous preparations to ensure that the feast would be much talked about and eagerly awaited. When the great day came, huge crowds, especially of Sabines, thronged to Rome, eager to have a look at the city. The visitors were shown all round. They saw the walls and the new buildings and they went to parties in the houses. They were most impressed to see how quickly Rome had grown. Then they all collected in the circus and the show began. As everyone was busy watching it a signal was suddenly given and the Romans attacked. Young men ran in and out among the crowd seizing all the girls and carrying them off. Most just took the first girls who came to hand, but certain particularly pretty ones had been earmarked for the chief men of the city, and these were led off under escort. The loveliest of all was taken by some men acting for a senator called Thalassius, and when people asked 'where are you taking her to?', they replied that no one was to touch her; 'she is for Thalassius' (and this is why at their wedding feasts the Romans for ever after used to shout 'Thalassio'). The show broke up in panic and the visitors fled from Rome, calling on the gods to punish the Romans for their monstrous treachery. The stolen girls were also in despair until Romulus went and spoke to them and explained that it was all their parents' fault for being so unco-operative. He promised them that they should marry Romans, and become citizens. 'Please don't be cross', he said, 'your anger will soon turn to love. Every man will try not only to be a good husband but to make up for the homes and parents you have lost.' And this in fact is what happened. The Romans were very kind and the Sabine girls were flattered by the attentions paid to them.

But the rest of the Sabines were by no means prepared to accept what had happened. An intolerable outrage had been committed and they had no intention of allowing it to go unpunished. Besides they had lost their wives and daughters and this was something that could not just be ignored. So for several years there was continual war between the Romans and the Sabines but in those far-off days their tactics and weapons were so primitive that it was difficult ever to reach a decisive result. There were endless scraps and skirmishes but no really full-scale battle. Two events, however, are worth remembering, though for different reasons.

The nearest the Sabines ever came to capturing Rome was when they managed to bribe Tarpeia the daughter of the commander of the Roman citadel to let a few armed soldiers secretly in. This had come about when Tarpeia went outside the walls to fetch some water for a religious service and met Tatius, the Sabine general, who was a strikingly handsome young man. Tarpeia fell in love with him at first sight and was so carried away that she promised to do anything he liked. She was also fascinated by the heavy gold

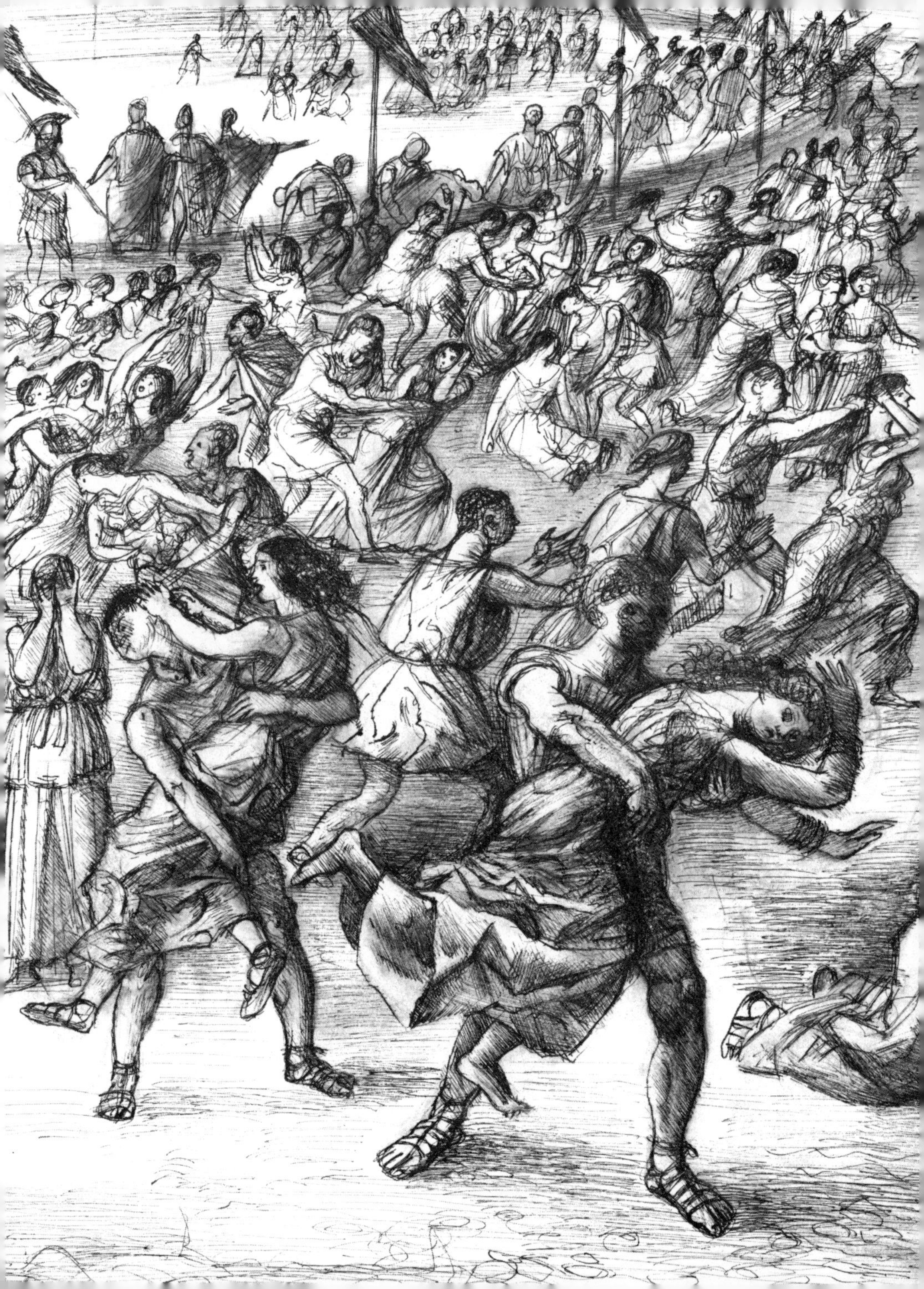

bracelets which the Sabines wore on their left arms. So it was arranged that she should betray Rome and should receive as payment 'what the soldiers had in their left hands'. But Tatius was only toying with her affections and as soon as his soldiers had gained an entrance they crushed her to death under the vast shields which they carried on their left arms. When the story leaked out, the Romans admitted that she had got what she deserved and they called part of the citadel 'the Tarpeian rock' after her.

The Tarpeian Rock today

In the meanwhile, however, the Sabines had control of the citadel and things looked very bad for the Romans. A desperate group of men under the command of Hostius Hostilius made one determined charge on it and for a while they carried everything before them against great odds. However when a stray shot hit Hostilius, they began to give ground and then turned tail and fled. Mettius Curtius, the captain of the Sabine detachment in the citadel, pursued them closely and it took all Romulus's courage and personality to rally the Romans and to lead them back to the fight, particularly now that the Sabines were flushed with success and were taunting them with cheap jibes. But the Sabines went too far; for Romulus was stung with anger when he heard someone shouting 'You can catch girls but you can't catch me' and threw himself into the fight with redoubled energy. It was now the turn of the Sabines to flee and this time the ground was in favour of the Romans. Mettius' retreat was cut off by a stretch of marsh and he looked round anxiously for another route. But there was none in sight, so amid the cheers of his own side he plunged into the marsh on his frightened horse. Miraculously he emerged safely at the other side and escaped back to the citadel.

Long after the war was over, the Romans recalled this exploit and named that part of the market-place where the marsh had been 'Curtius' Pond'.

Mettius Curtius

The trouble with the Sabines was the first of many disagreements with foreign powers. The next war that Rome was involved in was with her own mother-city Alba Longa, from which Romulus and Remus had originally come. We do not know the real reason for the ill feeling between the two states but the story of what happened was one of the most famous in Roman history.

The king of Rome at the time was Tullus Hostilius, the second king after Romulus, who reigned about 650 B.C. He was a hot-headed king who had much of Romulus' courage but lacked his wisdom and tact. The Albans had just got a new king, a weak young man, called Mettius Fufetius. He was particularly nervous because it was generally felt, that, whatever the reason, Alba was really responsible for the present war. So when Tullus proposed a conference to discuss a peaceful solution, Mettius readily agreed and the two kings met on neutral ground between their armies. In the discussions that followed both men admitted that the real issues were not the border incidents and cattle thieving that had been going on but were much larger. Both states were ambitious and felt cramped by their present frontiers; neither would be really satisfied until it had defeated the other. So Mettius suggested that instead of a full-scale battle between the Roman and Alban armies, in which inevitably many innocent lives would be lost, they should settle the matter by a battle of champions. Tullus welcomed this suggestion. It so happened that there were on each side three brothers serving in the ranks—three Curiatius brothers in the Alban army and three Horatii in the Roman. Since they were much of an age, it was agreed that the fate of the two countries should rest with them; whichever side should provide the winner should automatically be accepted by the other as master. The result of this match was to be final.

The rest of the two armies sat down in a vast circle to watch the six men fight it out. The atmosphere was tense and excited as the supporters on each side cheered their heroes into the centre; the future of whole countries was at stake and for the spectators the suspense was almost unbearable. There was a sudden blast from a trumpet at which the champions drew their swords and joined battle. For a long time no one could tell what was going on. In the confused

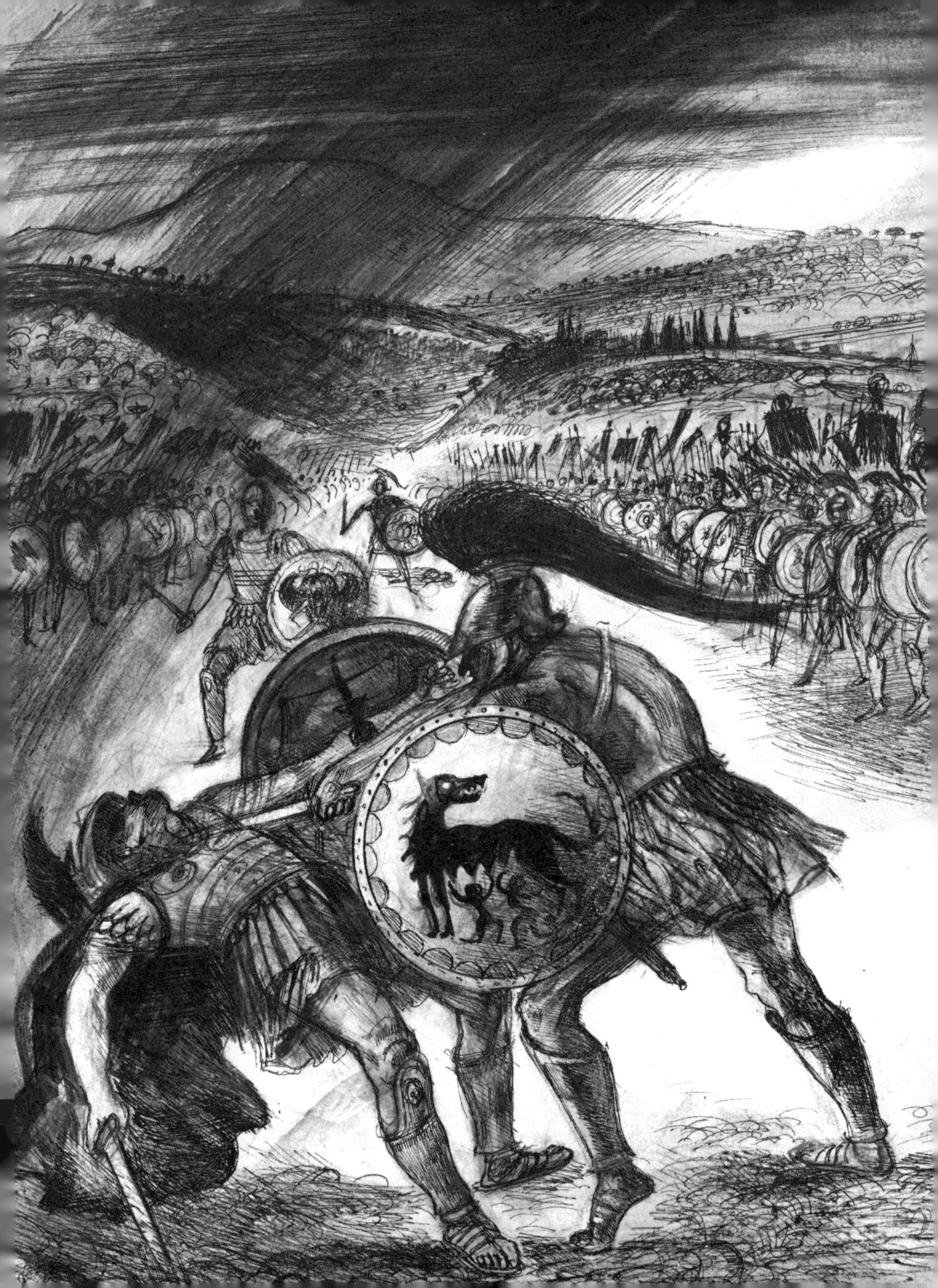

maul only the flash of swords and the sway of bodies could be seen. But then, as people held their breath, blood was seen to flow. First one Roman and then another slumped to the ground and lay still. A great shout rose up from the Albans, for victory seemed in their grasp, while the Romans were shocked into silence. But the last Horatius was quite unhurt while all three Curiatii were to some extent disabled by wounds which they had received in the course of the fight. Horatius saw at a glance that he was no match for all three of his opponents at once but he was confident that he could take them on individually. So he took to his heels and left the Curiatii to chase him as best they could. Gaps quickly appeared between them as they ran and Horatius had only to pause to strike down first one and then another as they caught up with him. At last it was one against one but with the difference that Horatius was still untouched whereas the remaining Curiatius was weak with loss of blood. It was all over in a moment. One blow left Horatius the winner and gave Rome control of Alba.

The relief in the Roman army was tremendous as they welcomed their champion back. The Albans accepted their defeat calmly and the two countries united to bury their dead in huge tombs which can still be seen to this day.

But the story had a sequel. Horatius's sister was engaged to one of the Curiatii and her feelings were sadly mixed as she watched her brother's triumphant entry into the city. Although she was proud of his victory and of Rome's success, she was as a woman deeply upset at the death of her fiancé. When she saw her brother carrying over his shoulders a cloak which she had made with her very own hands for Curiatius, she could bear it no longer and burst into tears. Horatius was annoyed at such a welcome from his own sister, which he took to be a sign of weakness. Seized by a wild impulse he stabbed her there and then with his dagger.

This murder caused much heart-searching among the Romans. On the one hand they could hardly let a murder go unpunished, on the other they were naturally reluctant to take action against the man who alone was responsible for their victory in the recent war. So they arrested him and held him in custody while they decided what to do. Luckily the priests were able to devise a religious compromise by which Horatius was absolved of the blood which he had shed by being made to walk, with his head covered, under a ceremonial arch, and was then set at liberty.

The peace, however, was too good to last. Mettius' position at Alba had been seriously undermined by his defeat and, in an attempt to bolster it up, he set about stirring up trouble for Rome among her neighbours. One of these cities, Fidenae, was induced to declare war on Rome in the hope that others would follow suit. Tullus promptly requested Mettius to provide an expeditionary force to help Rome in accordance with their agreement. Mettius duly turned up at the head of his men but instead of joining forces with the Romans he kept the Albans some distant apart, because he wanted to see which way things were going to go so that he could back the winner. When, therefore, the battle began, he quietly edged away and took up a neutral position on some low foothills. The Roman flank was thus exposed and for a while things looked desperate. Tullus, however, saw what was happening and made a split-second decision. He shouted out that there was nothing to worry about as the Albans were acting on his orders to outflank the enemy. This was heard both by the Romans who were at once encouraged by the news and by the enemy who began to look nervously over their shoulders to see what was happening. Tullus then seized the chance to press home his advantage and a single charge brought the battle to a speedy but bloody end.

Mettius hurried forward to congratulate Tullus on his success and was received politely by the king who proposed that they should camp where they were for the night and then tidy things up on the next day. However next morning, when the Alban and Roman armies came on parade, Tullus disarmed the Albans and put a guard round Mettius while he explained to the two armies how Mettius had planned to desert and betray the Romans, and how close to disaster they had been. He put the blame on Mettius and said that it was not the fault of the Albans who had only done their duty in obeying their king's orders. But Mettius was a traitor and should pay for it. Then turning to Mettius he spoke to him briefly: 'Yesterday your mind was divided and it was no doubt painful for you to decide whether to support the Romans or the Fidenates. Today it is your body that will be divided and I have no doubt that that will be even more painful for you.'

Two chariots, each drawn by four horses, were then led forward and Mettius's hands were tied to one, his feet to the other. On a crack of the whip the horses sprang forward in opposite directions and his body was torn in half. The sight was so frightful that nobody could bear to look at it. Indeed it was the first and only time in Roman history that such an inhuman punishment was inflicted; for it was one of the truest boasts of the Romans that they used only civilized and humane methods to enforce the laws.

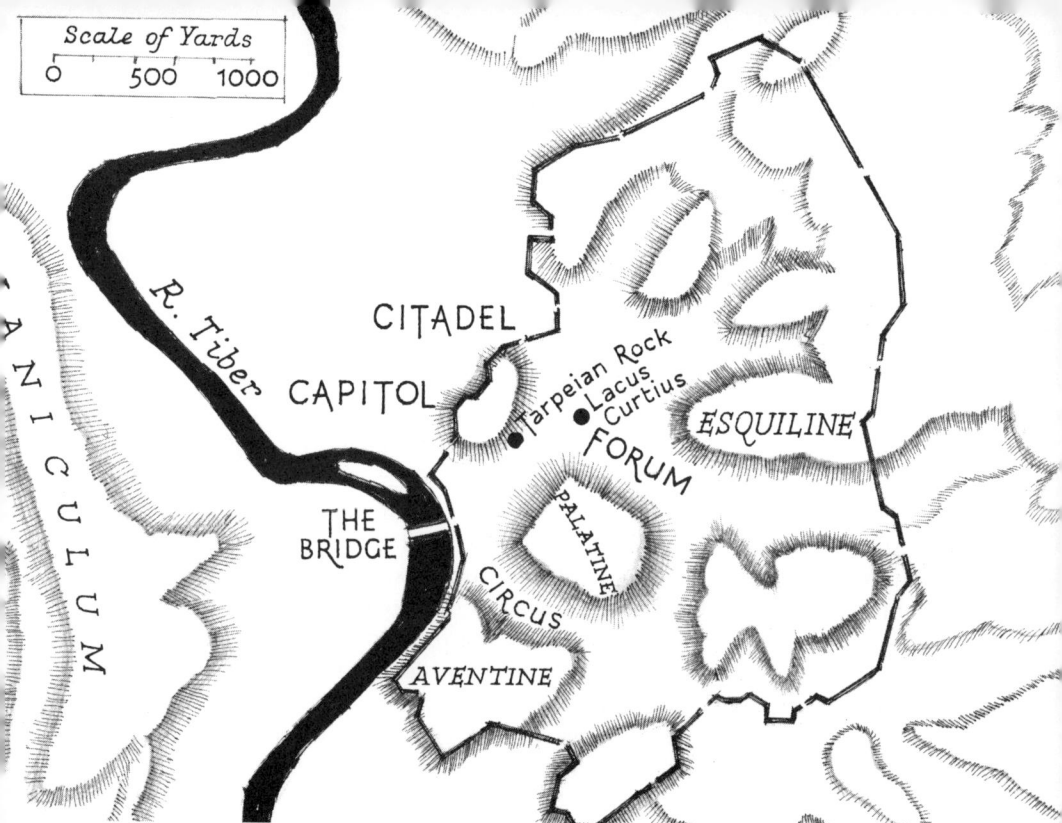

Plan of Rome

Rome became larger and more important. It had many advantages as a site for it was on the route by which salt was brought from the coast to the rest of Italy and it guarded one of the most important crossings of the River Tiber. It also lay on the border of several countries. There were Etruscans to the north, Sabines to the east and Latins to the south. Rome traded with all these people and grew rich as a result. But her main dealings were with the Etruscans, in particular the two cities of Caere and Veii which are about twenty miles north of Rome. By 600 B.C. many Etruscan merchants and craftsmen had come to live in Rome, thus bringing their civilization and their higher standard of living with them. Brick and stone buildings began to replace wooden huts; beautiful sculpture and metalwork were introduced for the first time. The Etruscans were more advanced than the Romans so that they soon took over the government of the city and chose their own kings.

Two Women

The first of these Etruscan kings was called Tarquin the Old. He had usurped the throne, when the last king died leaving two sons, the real heirs, still under age, but he had established his power so firmly that his right to the crown was soon unchallenged. He had reigned for many years, fighting successful wars against his neighbours and carrying on a steady rebuilding of the city, when a very extraordinary event occurred in his palace.

There was a little boy in the house named Servius Tullius, the son of a prisoner-of-war befriended by Tarquin's wife, Tanaquil. One evening Servius was asleep in his bed when his head suddenly seemed to catch fire. A number of people in the room saw the flames and began to scream until Tarquin and Tanaquil heard the noise and came running to see what was up. Just as they arrived, a servant brought a jug of water and was about to throw it on to the boy's hair to put out the fire, when Tanaquil stopped him and said that the boy should not be disturbed but should be allowed to sleep on until he woke up of his own accord. Sure enough, when he did open his eyes some minutes later, the fire went out and as far as could be seen had done him no harm at all.

Tanaquil took her husband quietly aside and explained that the flames must have been a miracle sent from heaven to show them that Servius was an exceptional boy who would one day bring great glory to the Tarquins and to Rome. Tarquin was taken in by her story and from that day onwards gave Servius the best education and treated him like one of his own children. Eventually he married his daughter to him and it became clear to everyone that Servius was to be the next king of Rome. This drove the two heirs to desperation. They had abandoned all hope of recovering their throne so long as Tarquin was alive but they had hoped that on his death they would be reinstated as the rightful princes. Now it seemed that Servius would be king and they would never regain their position. The situation called for violent remedies. They bribed two peasants to kill Tarquin, hoping that in the confusion that followed his death they would be able to outwit Servius, but they tried to make it appear the result of a sudden quarrel rather than a put-up job.

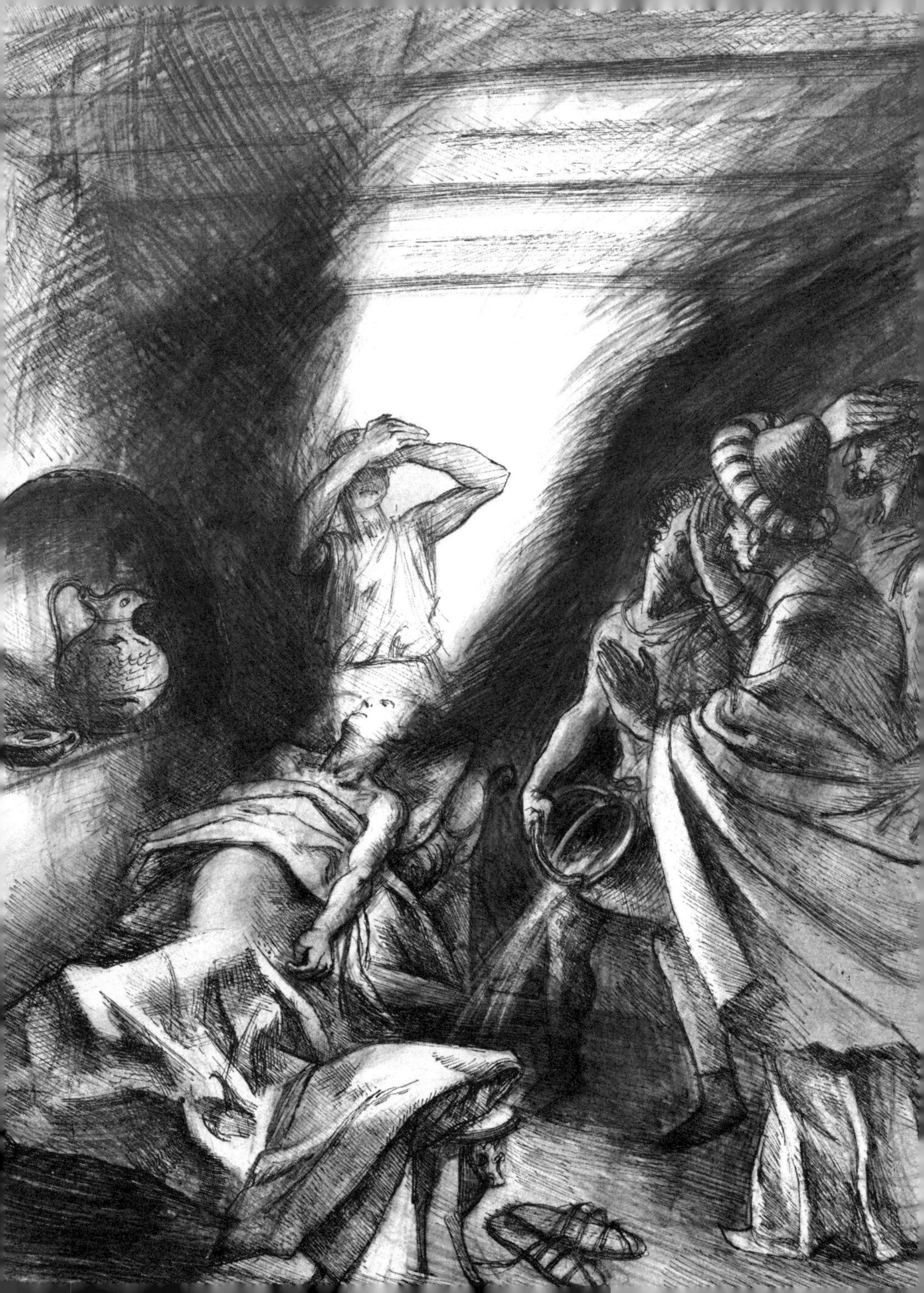

The two peasants, carrying axes as if they were about to go and chop some wood in the forest, met casually at the door of the palace and started an argument. This got louder and louder until it attracted the attention of Tarquin's attendants who dragged the couple before the king to settle their dispute for them. One of the peasants began to state his case and as the king devoted all his attention to him the other crept up behind him and felled him with his axe. The two men then made a dash for the door and tried to make good their escape.

In the chaos that followed only Tanaquil kept her head. She did what she could for her dying husband but when she saw that his case was hopeless she sent for Servius and urged him not to let the murder go unpunished. He saw that this was the chance for which he had been waiting and which had been foretold by the miracle when he was a boy. He agreed to hush up Tarquin's death until he secured his own position as king. In the meantime they would pretend that Tarquin was still alive and on the mend, and that he had asked Servius to take over the government until he was fully recovered. Having arranged this Tanaquil appeared on the palace balcony and addressed the vast crowd which had gathered anxiously in the streets round the palace. She calmed their fears by telling them that the blow had only stunned Tarquin and had proved on inspection to be a mere surface wound: the outlook was hopeful and the king had already recovered consciousness. She appealed to them meanwhile to take their orders from Servius who had been personally appointed by Tarquin as his deputy.

Tanaquil's presence of mind saved the day. The people returned to work and life went on as before. They accepted Servius without question and a few weeks later he felt strong enough to announce that Tarquin had relapsed and died. By then the two princes had lost heart and had gone to live abroad so that Servius succeeded automatically to the throne.

Servius' reign was long and prosperous. In the course of it he reorganised the Roman constitution and introduced new military tactics. But there were people in Rome who were jealous of him because, although he was a good king and although he had married Tarquin's daughter, they could not forget that he was not of royal blood but was merely a slave boy, the son of a prisoner-of-war. One of his most jealous enemies was his own son-in-law Lucius Tarquin who was to become the last king of Rome as Tarquin the Proud. Lucius and his brother Arruns were the young sons of Tarquin the Old. When they grew up, they had married Servius' daughters. The marriages were very ill-matched. Lucius was ambitious and energetic whereas his wife was easy-going. Arruns, on the other hand, had no ambitions, no desire to inherit the throne which had belonged to their father, but his wife, the other Tullia, longed to be a queen. She was humiliated that her husband showed so little spirit and she looked admiringly at the way in which Lucius, her brother-in-law, kept alive the claim of the Tarquins to be the true kings of Rome. Gradually their common interests drew Tullia and Lucius together. They began to plot secretly the overthrow of Servius but they realized that the main obstacle to their plans was the cowardice of the other two. How much better it would have been if Tullia had married Lucius instead of Arruns! As it was they decided that the best thing to do was to get rid of the others and two quick murders left the way open for them to get married.

All was now ready for the final attack on the aged Servius. Tullia nagged Lucius continually to take action and to show himself worthy of his royal blood by deposing Servius and reigning in his stead. At last she overcame his doubts and scruples and he set about collecting a group of supporters among the upper-class youths. Many of them had large gambling debts which he promised to pay if he became king. Others he bribed with offers of good jobs in the government. Some were Etruscans like himself and had always remained loyal to the House of Tarquin. Soon he had a large enough following to seize a moment when Servius was at home and to march into the market-place with his men. There, sitting on the king's throne in front of the Senate House, he was proclaimed King Tarquin by a herald. He summoned the councillors and proceeded to denounce Servius as a usurper who had no respect for birth or property, but, even as he was speaking, a rumour of what had happened brought Servius hurrying to the scene. A bitter slanging match took place during which the feelings of the crowd were divided, some shouting for Tarquin, some for Servius. At this critical moment Tarquin saw that his only hope was to take extreme measures. He stepped forward, seized Servius bodily in his arms and threw him down the steps. This piece of violence shocked the crowd into silence and they left Servius to creep home, bruised and battered and alone. But he never reached home. Tarquin sent some thugs after him who beat him up and left him dead in the street.

So twice in Roman history a forceful woman had put a king on the throne. But Tullia outdid Tanaquil in ruthlessness. For as she was driving home in her coach after congratulating Tarquin on his success, she met the corpse of her father lying bleeding in the road. The horses shied and the coachman tried to turn back, but Tullia snatched the reins from his hands and callously drove over her dead father, spattering her clothes and the coach with blood. The memory of this bestial deed was never forgotten by the Romans who re-named the street 'the Street of Crime'.

The Fall of Gabii

Tarquin, the new king of Rome, was a cruel ruler in peace but he was not bad as a general in wartime. A war had broken out with Gabii, a nearby town, which turned out to be unexpectedly difficult. Tarquin attacked the town in force but it held out against him. Then he besieged it, but this was not successful either since the Gabines drove him away from the walls. So, in the end, he decided to win the town by a trick, although this was a most un-Roman thing to do. He pretended that he had given up trying to take the town and went back to Rome. In the meantime he let his youngest son, Sextus, desert to Gabii on the excuse that he had been bullied by his father. The Gabines welcomed the deserter—'It is not surprising', they said, 'that Tarquin is cruel to his children; he has always been a tyrant'.

Sextus soon managed to get himself a place on the Gabine Council. On the whole he was very humble and said he agreed with the Councillors who were older than himself and who knew more about Gabine affairs. But on one thing he insisted that he knew best. Over and over again he urged them to go to war. The Gabines began to think that perhaps he was right for, after all, he did know the strength of both nations and had inside information about the poor state of Roman morale. So, bit by bit, he persuaded the Gabines to renew the war and to permit him to lead small raiding parties. These battles, which he had arranged in advance with his father that the Gabines should be allowed to win, proved so successful that the troops came to trust him entirely and made him commander-in-chief.

When Sextus realized that he was now as powerful in Gabii as his father was in Rome, he sent one of his trusty followers to Rome to ask his father what he would like him to do. Tarquin did not dare give the messenger a written message in case it should fall into enemy hands. He did not dare even to give him a spoken message. Instead the king walked up and down in the garden as if he was deep in thought. The messenger was surprised to see that as he passed silently up and down he kept cutting off the heads of the tallest poppies with his stick. In the end, the messenger got tired

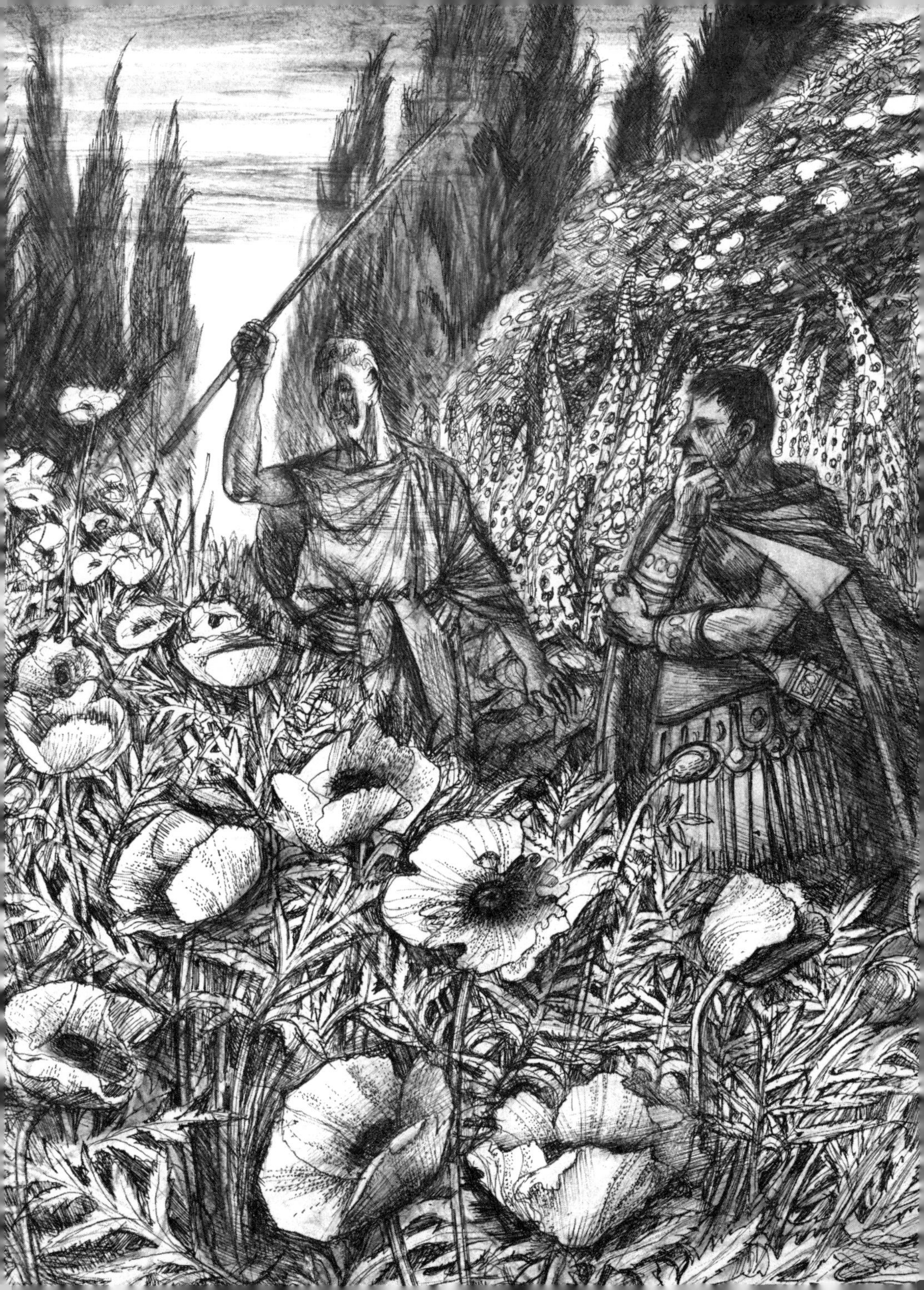

of waiting for an answer and when he returned to Gabii reported to Sextus that he was afraid that he had failed in his mission as the king had not said a word. However, when he told Sextus what Tarquin had been doing in the garden Sextus realized that this was the message. He had the chief men of Gabii murdered and then confiscated their property to bribe the poorer classes. Thereby he destroyed all their patriotism and independence, so that he was soon able to hand over Gabii to his father without a struggle.

The Expulsion of the Tarquins

This success proved in the end the undoing of the Tarquins. King Tarquin became more and more ambitious, wanting to capture all the surrounding cities while his son Sextus was so pleased with himself that he thought he could do anything he liked. Tarquin decided to attack the city of Ardea next, which lay about twenty miles south of Rome. When his first assault failed, he settled down to besiege it in the usual way. Sieges are always boring and while the troops had to man the trenches the officers found themselves with a lot of time on their hands, which they whiled away with parties. One evening somebody started a competition to decide who had the best wife. Everyone sang the praises of his own wife and the competition became quite heated until one of the officers called Collatinus suggested that it could be easily settled if they rode to Rome on the spur of the moment and saw what each of their wives was doing. The idea appealed to them and they jumped on their horses. When they got to Rome they found that in their absence all their wives, with the exception of Lucretia, Collatinus' wife, had gone off to dinners and dances with other men. Lucretia was quietly sitting at home with her domestic servants knitting by candlelight. So Lucretia won the competition.

But Sextus was infatuated by the sight of Lucretia's beauty and a few days later he returned to her house late at night. He was invited in and given a meal and a bed. He waited until he thought that everyone would be asleep and it would be safe to move. Then he slipped out of the door with a drawn sword and made his way to Lucretia's bedroom. He woke her gently with his hand and told

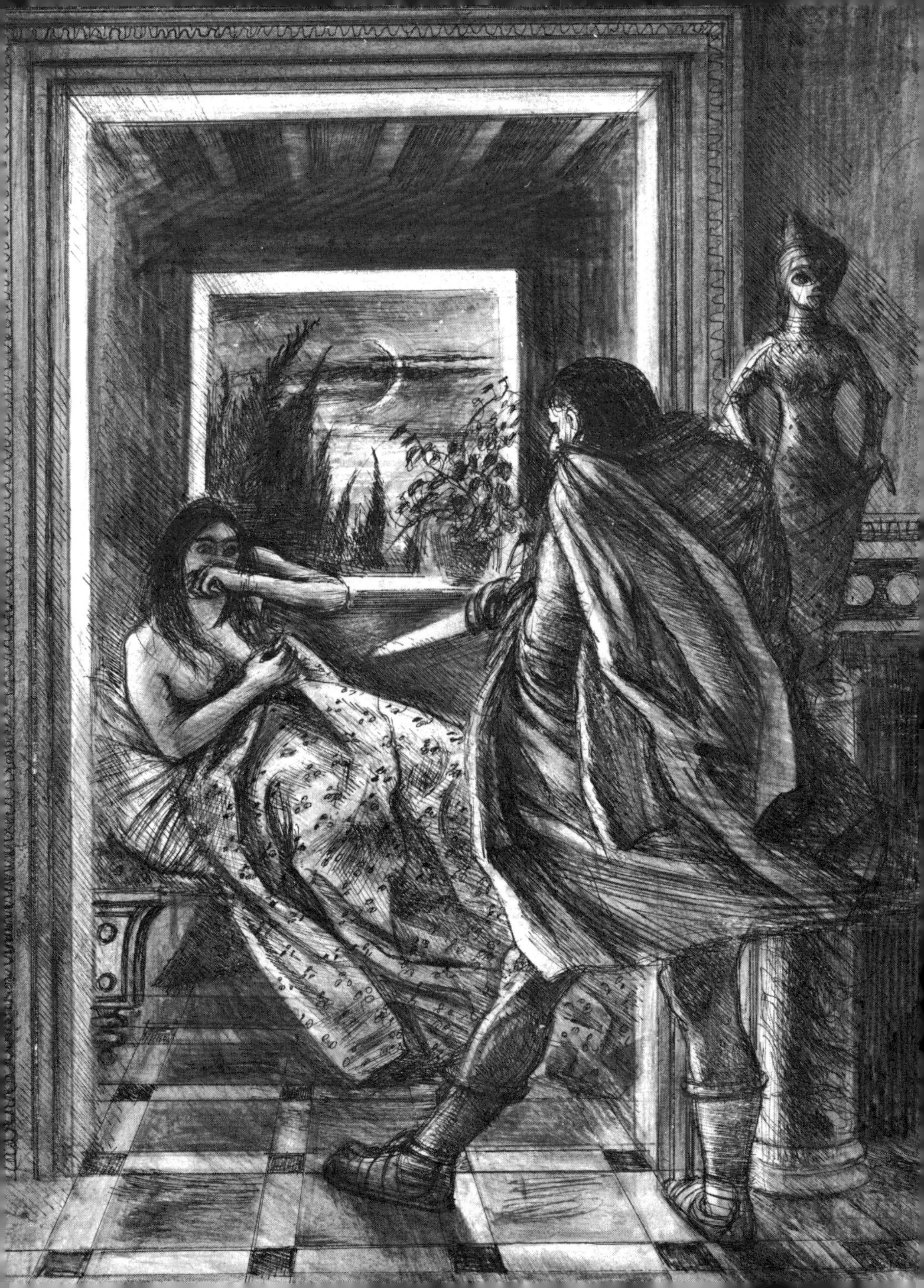

her who he was and said that he wanted her for himself, warning her not to make the slightest noise on pain of death. Lucretia was terrified but, when she saw that she was alone and helpless, she used every argument she could think of to get rid of him. But it was no good. Sextus was adamant and even threatened, if she didn't give way, to kill a slave in bed with her so that it would look as if she had been caught in a thoroughly sordid affair. Lucretia broke down and wept. There was nothing more that she could do to prevent him having his way with her.

Next day she sent a message to her father and to her husband Collatinus, asking them to come as quickly as possible with two trusty friends because there had been a terrible disaster. They came at once, bringing Publius Valerius and Lucius Junius Brutus with them, and found her crying in her room. When they asked what was the matter, she explained what had happened, how she had been betrayed by Sextus who had abused the welcome she had innocently given him. She swore that she would prove by her death that, although her body had been violated, her heart was pure and she made them swear not to allow Sextus' villainy to go unpunished. The men agreed to avenge her but tried to reason with her, arguing that it was not her fault and that she had done nothing wrong. But Lucretia would not be dissuaded. She did not want to give an excuse for other girls to go wrong. She had hidden a dagger in her clothes and plunging it into her heart she fell forwards—dead.

Her father and her husband cried out in horror and, as they stood numbed at her feet, Brutus plucked the dagger from the wound and holding it in front of him, dripping with blood, he took a solemn oath to remove from Rome all the Tarquins and their relations by every means in his power. Then he passed the dagger to Collatinus, and next to Lucretius and Valerius, who all repeated his words. After that they carried Lucretia's body to the marketplace, where a vast crowd gathered in shocked silence to watch. Brutus seized the moment to work on their anger and pity. In an inspired speech he incited them to join him in armed rebellion against the Tarquins and within a few weeks Tarquin the Proud was forced to resign his throne and flee to Caere with his family, except for Sextus who unwisely went to Gabii where the memory of his treachery was so bitter that he was arrested and summarily executed.

That was the end of the Etruscan kings at Rome. In their place the Romans created a government of chief magistrates, called consuls, who were elected democratically every year. But they had not heard the last of the Tarquins, who made strenuous efforts to recover their throne.

Horatius Cocles

When Tarquin was expelled from Rome, he went first to Caere and then took refuge with Lars Porsenna, King of Clusium. Porsenna was also an Etruscan by birth so that Tarquin was able to appeal to their common ties of family and race and to persuade him to launch a military expedition to put him back on the throne of Rome. Besides, Porsenna was afraid that the habit of deposing kings might spread and that even he might lose his kingdom, one of the finest ever seen. So he agreed to help Tarquin and marched with a great army on Rome. The Romans fled from the countryside at his approach and manned the walls of the city, but there was one weak spot in the defences. There was a bridge over the river Tiber which gave access to a neighbouring hill, called the Janiculum. This hill had been fortified with a small outpost but when the outpost was captured by a surprise attack, the Roman defenders turned and ran, leaving the way open to the bridge. If it had not been for the courage and presence of mind of one man, Horatius Cocles, in that crisis, Rome must have been captured too. He happened to be on guard-duty on the bride when the Janiculum was seized. As the Romans rushed down the hill in confusion and fled across the bridge to the safety of the city, he did his best to rally them, desperately warning them that, if the bridge fell into enemy hands, nothing could stop the Etruscans from entering Rome. 'You must break down the bridge behind me', he shouted, 'while I hold up the enemy advance.' With resolute strides, he made his way to the head of the bridge, accompanied by two brave and noble companions, Spurius Larcius and Titus Herminius. Side by side they held the Etruscan attacks at bay, until they heard a shout that the bridge was almost cut through. Horatius then ordered the other two to make for safety while he covered their retreat on his own. For a moment the Etruscans were so surprised at his nerve that they held their fire but, when they recovered, they charged in a mass on him. They attacked him with all their weapons but still Horatius was able to bar their way single-handed. At last a sudden cheer from the other side of the river told him that the bridge had been destroyed and with a prayer for safe passage he jumped into the Tiber.

Horatius and the bridge

Miraculously he swam unharmed through a hail of arrows and spears to the other bank where the Romans greeted him as a hero. Rome was saved. And in recognition of his services he was given as much land as he could plough round in a day.

The Etruscans now began to blockade Rome. No supplies could enter the town and since there was little food in Rome (and that expensive) Porsenna hoped that he would conquer Rome without having to fight a battle. However, a young Roman noble, Gaius Mucius, felt that it was quite wrong that the Romans should be cooped up in this way when they could easily beat the Etruscans in the field. So he planned a bold stroke. At first he thought he would steal into the enemy's camp without telling anyone, but then he was afraid that the Roman sentries would see him and accuse him of trying to desert, so he consulted the Senate first and got their permission. Hiding a sword under his clothes, he made his way into the enemy camp and joined the crowd around the royal tribunal.

It was pay-day for the Etruscan troops and the royal paymaster, dressed in a splendid uniform, was sitting next to the king paying out money and answering all the soldiers' questions. Mucius could not decide which of the two men on the tribunal was the king and he did not like to ask for fear of betraying himself. So he decided to take a chance and drawing his sword he sprang forwards. But by ill luck he killed the paymaster instead of the king.

There was a shocked silence during which he tried to make his escape, brandishing his bloody sword, but the royal guard, recovering quickly, caught him and dragged him before the king. Even then—alone, and at the Etruscan's mercy—he spoke fearlessly: 'I am a Roman citizen', he said, 'my name is Gaius Mucius. I am your enemy and I would kill you if I could, but, having failed, I am quite prepared to die bravely like a Roman. Let me warn you, however, that I am not the only Roman who will try to kill you. Behind me is a queue of nobles competing for that honour. So be prepared. Your life is in danger every hour and there will always be someone after your blood.'

The king was so angry at Mucius's impertinence that he ordered him to be burnt alive, but Mucius was unmoved by this threat. To show that he didn't care, he calmly put his right hand into the fire which was burning on an altar nearby. The king could not help admiring such courage, even in an enemy, and he ordered him to be released at once and given a safe-conduct back to Rome. So Mucius returned to Rome and ever afterwards was nicknamed Scaevola, which means left-handed, because he had voluntarily destroyed his right hand.

Mucius's brave deed fired the men of Rome with patriotism. Cloelia showed that the women too could be courageous. The Romans had made a temporary treaty with Porsenna and as one of the conditions had handed over a number of hostages to the Etruscans. Cloelia was one of them. One day, when the Etruscans camped near the Tiber, Cloelia escaped with a group of girls. They swam across the river and despite a fusillade of Etruscan fire they all got over safely and made their way to Rome. The king was furious when he learnt of this escape. He didn't care much about the other girls, but he demanded the return of Cloelia as the ringleader. However, when he was told the full details his anger gave way to admiration for such heroism which outdid even Horatius and Mucius. He told the Romans that if the hostages were not handed back he would consider the treaty broken, but that if they sent Cloelia back he would let her go home unharmed.

So Cloelia went back to the Etruscan camp and appeared before the king. He praised her heroism and offered to let her choose half the hostages to go back to Rome with her. She very sensibly chose the young boys.

37

After the war was over the Romans made a statue of Cloelia sitting on a horse and put it up on the summit of the Sacred Way and it remained there for hundreds of years to remind the Romans of her.

In the years that followed the withdrawal of Porsenna and his Etruscans from the gates of the city, Rome grew in size and power. But she had always two dangers to watch out for. At this time there were a number of tribes, such as the Volsci and the Aequi, who were roaming in central Italy, looking for easy targets to attack. But these foreign enemies were not as serious as the traitors within Rome itself who tried to overthrow the Republic. These dangers were shown by what happened to Coriolanus.

The Story of Coriolanus

His real name was Gnaeus Marcius. He was a young, proud Roman nobleman who was a commander in the Roman army which was waging war on the Volscians. While the Romans were besieging the Volscian city of Corioli and, over-confident as usual, were keeping only a slack look-out, there was a sudden sally from the garrison inside the city supported by an attack by a commando division on the rear. Alone among the Roman generals Marcius kept his head, and with a picked band he forced his way through the opened gate of the fortress and hurled a firebrand into a crowded part of the city close to the walls. There was a general panic among the citizens and Corioli fell to the Romans. Ever afterwards Marcius was known as Coriolanus in honour of his bravery that day.

Unfortunately his success seems to have gone to his head. His natural arrogance increased. He resented the growing power of the common people and disliked the way their leaders were insisting on selling food cheaply to them in order to gain their support. He took every opportunity of abusing these men in public until they could bear it no longer. So, to prevent the people taking the law into their own hands and murdering him in cold blood, the

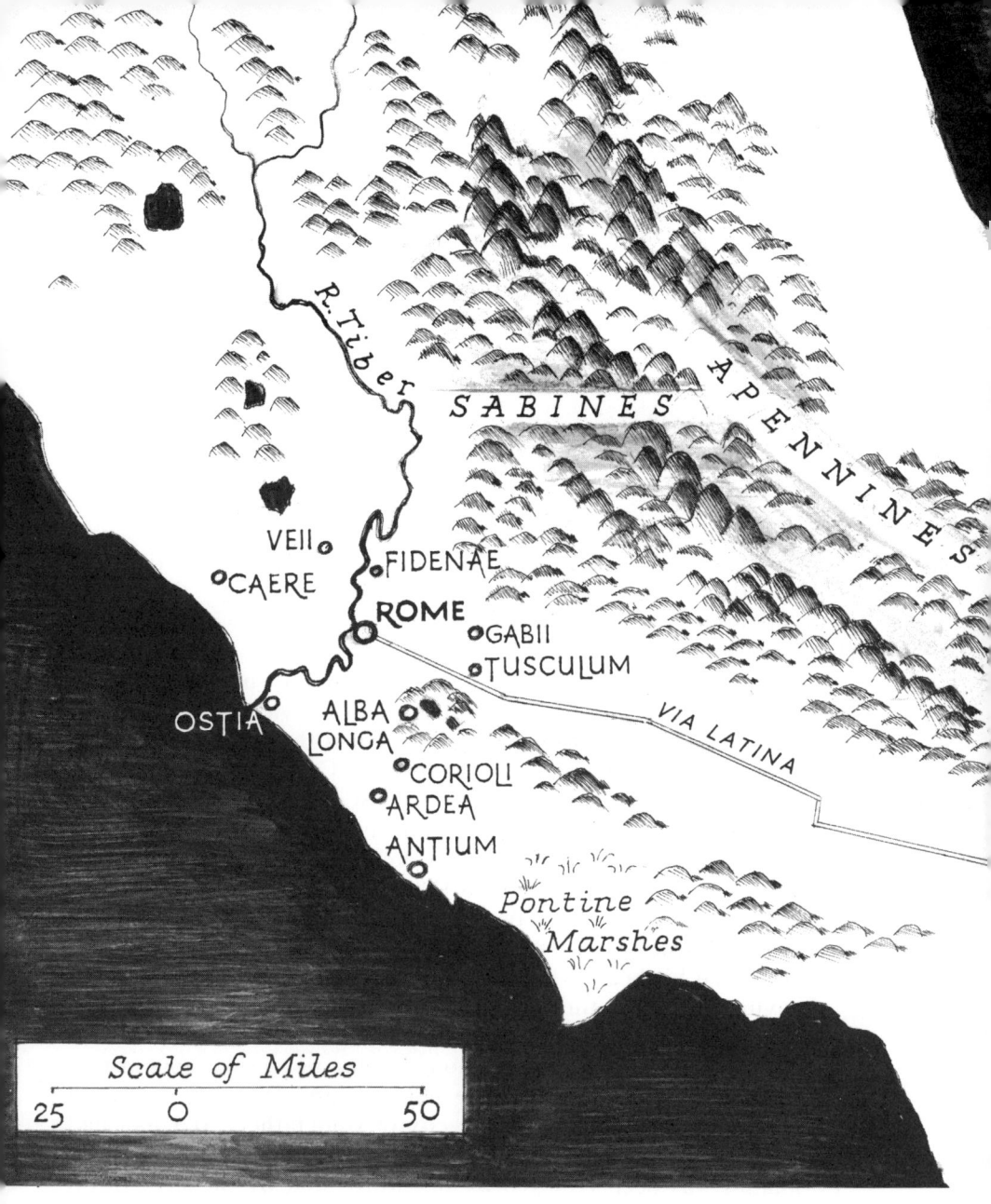

The surroundings of Rome and Corioli

Senate summoned Coriolanus to appear before them on a fixed day. He sent no apology and did not even turn up to defend himself. It is not surprising that he was banished from Rome.

In a fury, Coriolanus went straight to Antium, the headquarters of the Volscian army, and offered them his services. He quickly rose to power and never ceased to urge a new attack on Rome. An opportunity for this soon came. The Roman Senate decided to order a replay of the Games and to hold them in circumstances of great splendour. Crowds of Volscians journeyed to Rome to join in the celebrations. Acting on instructions from Coriolanus, one of the Volscian leaders secretly persuaded the Romans that the presence of so many ex-enemies in the capital was a danger to the peace. So an order was sent out from the Roman Senate commanding all Volscians to leave Rome immediately and to return home. The Volscians were furious at missing the Games in this undignified way and at this lack of trust in their good behaviour. When they got back to their own country they clamoured for revenge. Coriolanus had no difficulty in raising an army, with himself in command, to march on Rome.

The campaign went well from the start. Many towns were captured and the land ravaged and laid waste. When the victorious army was within five miles from Rome the city seemed doomed, and in their panic the Roman Senate sent envoys to Coriolanus begging for mercy. These he treated with the utmost disdain. Nor would he listen to the priests who waited on him dressed in all their splendid vestments. At last, in despair, the women of Rome summoned an emergency meeting and persuaded Veturia his mother, and Volumnia his wife with their two little boys to march with them to the enemy's camp and throw themselves on his mercy. Perhaps they would be able to soften his heart when all others had failed.

Leaving the city, the group of women slowly approached the victorious Volscian army. Coriolanus saw them coming and when he was told his mother was among them, he rushed forward to embrace her. But she would have none of him. 'You are no son of mine' she said 'for you attack the city of your fathers. If I had had no son, instead of a traitor, Rome today would not be in peril.' Coriolanus was deeply moved by her words and by the sight of his wife and children. He broke down completely and withdrew his army from the gates of Rome.

But that was not the end of the story. Coriolanus was now deeply hated by the Volscians as well as by the Romans. He was disgraced and all his wealth and honours taken from him. Some say he was put to death, others that he died in poverty and misery—an exile in a strange land. Only his name—Coriolanus—remains to remind us of his vanished glory.

Cremera

As Rome became more powerful and extended her frontiers, the neighbouring cities began to fear the effects of her aggression. One city in particular felt that she was being threatened. This was Veii, which, like Rome, lay close to the river Tiber and commanded the trade routes which led from the ports on the coasts to the great markets of central Italy. Veii was a rich and large city, peopled by Etruscans. It was situated on a wide plateau surrounded by steep precipices so that it could only be approached along a narrow neck of land from the north and it was heavily guarded. The strength

Veii

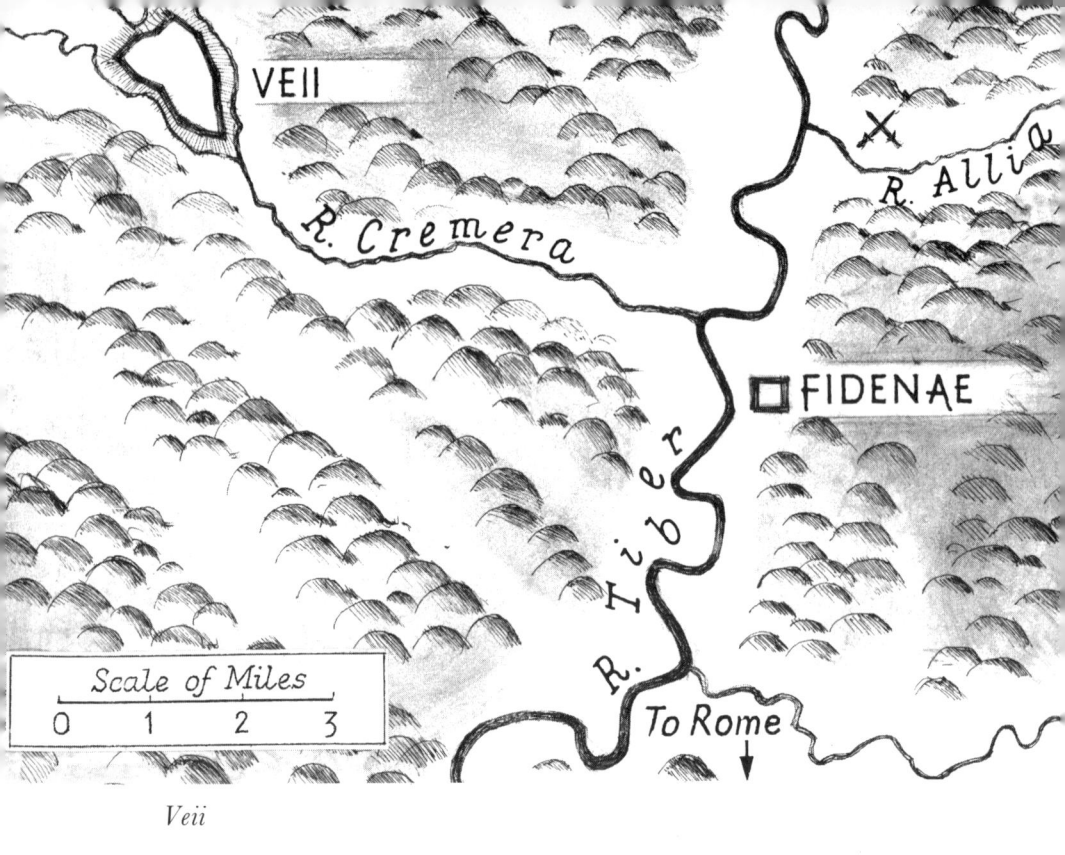

of its position enabled the inhabitants, Veientanes as they were called, to make sudden attacks on the Roman countryside and to damage Roman trade. These attacks became so frequent and so troublesome that the Romans decided that they would have to build some forts to stop the Veientanes from invading them and to protect their land. But Rome was short of troops, particularly because she had to keep other armies ready to face attacks from other enemies to the east and south of the city. In this crisis, the leaders of a single family, the Fabii, volunteered to provide at their own cost a permanent garrison to patrol the Veii frontier. Their offer was accepted with enthusiasm and the Fabii were warmly thanked for coming to the rescue of Rome. One morning the whole family, 306 in number, with their servants and dependants, paraded in the forum under the command of their chieftain, Caeso Fabius, and prepared to march out and pitch their camp on the borders between Rome and Veii. It was a splendid sight and the crowd that had gathered to see them off wished them every success and promised to reward them richly on their return. But their departure was spoiled by a strange incident. By mistake they left the city through the right-hand side of the city gates, which was always regarded as being unlucky.

At first, however, all seemed to be well. The Fabii fortified a small post on the river Cremera, which led from Veii to the Tiber. There they were able to intercept any Veientane army that tried to enter Roman territory and, as a result, there was peace all along the frontier between Rome and Veii. Even when the Etruscans brought up a large force to make a direct attack on the fort, they were beaten back with heavy losses. This made the Veientanes more cautious and more cunning. Instead of fighting the Fabii openly, they tried to catch them off their guard. They left herds of cattle unattended in the fields and evacuated their farms. This tempted the Fabii to come out from the safety of their fort in order to seize whatever they could lay their hands on. Gradually the Fabii became careless and over-confident until at last they made a rash expedition to capture some flocks which they had caught sight of a long way from the Cremera. They were hurrying along in twos and threes, chasing the sheep which had scattered as sheep do, when the Veientanes suddenly emerged from an ambush in which they were hiding, and surrounded them. The Romans were helpless. Completely outnumbered and encircled they broke and ran as the Etruscans fired at them from every side. They managed to fight their way through to a little hill where they regrouped to make a last, desperate stand. Even here they might have survived, if the Veientanes had not discovered a secret path which led them round under cover to take the Fabii in the rear. This was the final blow. The hill was captured and the Fabii were killed to a man, all 306 of them. Only one Fabius is said to have survived. He was a little boy who had been left at home because he was too young, but he lived to be the ancestor of the great Fabius Maximus Cunctator who was to save Rome in the darkest hours of the war against Hannibal.

Cincinnatus

Not all the great Roman generals were rich and aristocratic. One of the most famous was a poor man called Cincinnatus who owned a small four-acre farm across the river Tiber. One day, as he was busy ploughing, he was surprised to see some messengers from the Roman Senate approaching him across his fields. He called to his wife Racilla to bring his cloak from their cottage. 'Is all well?' he asked them.

They told him why they had come. The enemy was threatening Rome and laying waste the surrounding countryside. A Roman army under one of the consuls had fallen into a trap and was completely encircled. Things looked desperate. The Senate had sent them to invite Cincinnatus to become dictator and to save his country.

Cincinnatus did not hesitate. He crossed the river in the boat which was standing ready for him. Once in Rome he quickly took over the supreme command. He appointed as second in command another poor man, Lucius Tarquitius, who in spite of his ability and noble birth, had not been able to afford a commission in the army. A state of emergency was proclaimed and all shops were closed. General conscription was ordered and every able-bodied man had to report for duty bringing with him provisions for five days. The older men had to provide food for the soldiers. Cincinnatus told his new army exactly what had happened and why great speed was necessary if their fellow-countrymen were to be rescued. His enthusiasm was infectious and the men responded magnificently to his challenge. As they drew near the beleaguered army they gave a great shout which penetrated to the encircled men and encouraged them to try to fight their way out again. The enemy were surprised by their sallies and fell back on the well-entrenched troops of Cincinnatus. Soon they were pleading for mercy. Cincinnatus was anxious to prevent a general massacre. He sent the enemy generals in chains to Rome. Each enemy soldier had to pass under a yoke of three spears, symbolic of their utter humiliation and utter defeat.

Cincinnatus returned to Rome in triumph, at the head of his victorious army. But he did not want further honour and glory for himself nor a life of ease. Six months after being appointed dictator, he resigned and once more crossed the river to go back to his little farm.

On the whole, despite frequent alarms, Rome prospered during the first sixty years of the Republic but about 450 B.C. things took a turn for the worse. Food was scarce; money was short; the crops had failed for two years running and there were several epidemics in the city. On top of all this Rome had two serious wars on her hands at the same time. The lower classes were increasingly critical of the way in which the government was handling the situation. It seemed to them that the consuls were more interested in their own personal affairs than in what was happening to the country as a whole and this was strikingly proved by a tragic event that occurred in this year.

Verginia

Lucius Verginius, a sergeant in the Roman Army, had a very beautiful young daughter called Verginia. She was engaged to marry an ambitious young revolutionary leader called Lucius Icilius. Unfortunately Appius Claudius, one of the consuls, happened to see her in the street one day and fell in love with her at first sight. She refused to have anything to do with him, in spite of all his wealth and power. This maddened Appius and made him more determined than ever to marry her. As he could not win her by fair means, he made a dastardly plot to capture her. He told one of his officers, Marcus Claudius, to claim the girl as his slave. He counted on being able to get away with this villainy since her father was serving with the army away from home.

Verginia was seized in the market place on the way to school. She was speechless with terror but the cries of her maid soon collected a crowd round the unfortunate girl and all were on her side. Marcus saw he must change his tactics. He at once said the girl was in no danger but that she must be prepared to defend her case in court, to prove she was born free.

When the day for hearing the charge came, imagine the horror of her supporters when they saw that the judge who was to hear the case was none other than the wicked Appius himself.

In the absence of her father, Verginia was defended by Icilius, the man she had promised to marry. He made a moving and passionate speech urging Appius to postpone judgement till the girl's father should arrive.

Appius said he would adjourn the case for one day only. At the same time he secretly sent a message to the sergeant's company commander telling him on no account to give Verginius leave to attend the court. Verginius, however, had already obtained leave and was on his way to Rome.

He reached the market place as Appius was re-opening the case. Appius was furious to see him there and, in spite of the obvious anger of the crowd, he refused to listen to the distracted father's plea for mercy. Nor would he respect his rights as a citizen and a soldier to protect his daughter's honour. He proceeded at once to give judgement against Verginius and to hand over Verginia to Marcus as a slave.

Pandemonium at once broke out in the crowd but Appius, having foreseen trouble, had taken the precaution of bringing a company of troops with him to enforce order. These armed men pushed the citizens aside and seized the wretched girl. Her father, seeing that all was lost, grasped a knife from a butcher in the crowd, and plunged it into his daughter's heart.

Then the fury of the crowd knew no bounds—in their anger and distress they turned on Appius who fled for his life. In disguise he sought shelter in a friend's house. From then his public career was over. All his honours and power were taken from him and he went into exile. But the lovely Verginia was dead and her father and lover were left with only the memory of her dazzling and fatal beauty.

The death of Verginia had some good results. The constitution was reformed to make it more truly democratic and a Commission was appointed to codify and publish the laws which came to be known as the Twelve Tables. This helped to put Rome back on her feet, because the people could see that they were getting a fair deal and could trust the government. But there was one more storm to weather before the city settled down and the class struggles could be forgotten.

Sp. Maelius

It had been another poor harvest which led to a serious shortage of food in the city. Everybody blamed everybody else. The government said that the workers were idle and that the farmers should stay on their farms instead of wasting their time with political meetings or the attractions of the city. The poor put the blame on the government's bungling and mis-management. Eventually there was general agreement that one man should be given special powers to reorganize the food supplies and L. Minucius was given the job. Minucius began by sending round to all the cities in the neighbourhood and asking them to sell corn. He was able to get a little from Etruria but, apart from this, his mission was unsuccessful. So instead he was forced to introduce a system of rationing in Rome to ensure fair shares. He also prohibited hoarding and took strong action against the black market but these measures did little to help the poor and only showed up the extent of the problem. People tightened their belts and hoped for the best. But as time went by and things deteriorated, there was an alarming rise in the suicide rate.

In this tense situation a wealthy business-man called Sp. Maelius saw a chance of exploiting things to his profit. He had bought up a large supply of corn from private sources which he started distributing free to the poor. This was quite unofficial but naturally it won him immense popularity so that before long he was cheered and mobbed wherever he went. With this backing Maelius planned to challenge the government. His ambition was not just to be consul. He wanted to be king. Nothing less would satisfy him.

His plans were carefully laid. A constant stream of agents, many of them corn-dealers, came and went to his house and reported on how things were developing. In a short while the time would be ripe to strike. Fortunately, however, word of the plot came to the ears of Minucius who at once reported to the Senate that there was trouble afoot and that Maelius was collecting a great store of arms and ammunition in his house. The news startled the Senate, because they had enough problems on their hands without having to worry about an armed insurrection, but they decided that desperate ills needed desperate remedies and that they should call the aged Cincinnatus from retirement and hand over supreme command to him. This was a sensible decision; for Cincinnatus was a man of experience and courage, and in a crisis like this it would have been fatal to hesitate. Cincinnatus reluctantly agreed to serve and chose Caius Servilius Ahala as his adjutant. His first act was to set up road-blocks throughout the city and to station patrols in all the main streets. Then he proceeded to the market-place where the people had gathered, waiting nervously to see what was going to happen. It was an impressive sight, as Cincinnatus, now well over eighty, moved slowly into the centre of the great crowd and gazed sternly around him. For a moment he paused. Then he ordered Servilius to summon Maelius before him. Maelius paled and shrank back, asking the reason for the summons. Servilius replied that Minucius had accused him of treason and that the charge would have to be answered before a court of inquiry. For a moment Maelius toyed with the idea of bluffing his way out and pretending that he was completely innocent. But his nerve failed. He shook off the officer who was about to arrest him and took to his heels, hoping that the crowd would protect him. He did not get far. Servilius overtook him and cut him down on the spot.

When Servilius, still stained with blood, returned to Cincinnatus and reported that he had killed Maelius for attempting to resist arrest and for inciting a revolt, the dictator congratulated him on having saved the country from anarchy. This was the last occasion for many years on which the internal security of Rome was seriously threatened—which was just as well as there were many other things to occupy her attention.

The Fall of Veii

As the years went by, it became clear that Veii and Rome could not co-exist together. One or other of them had to be eliminated because their rivalry led to endless disputes and tensions. When the great war eventually came, which was to last for ten whole years— as long as the Trojan war—no one expected that it would be so savage or so drawn out. But at an early stage the Romans realized that if they were to have any chance of success, they would have to conduct a kind of trench-war all year long in order to blockade Veii and prevent it receiving supplies or reinforcements from its allies. So the Roman generals decided to continue the siege during the winter and to build winter quarters for the Roman troops in the field. This was a quite new thing which roused great misgivings at home. The popular leaders claimed that it was all a trick to keep the soldiers at the front away from home so that they should not be able to have any say in politics. But the Roman government succeeded in convincing them that total war was their only hope and that although the soldiers might have to put up with hard conditions

The walls of Veii today

at the front—harder even than the Veientanes had to endure—it was necessary if they were to win a decisive victory. But despite all these efforts the war still did not seem to go well. On one occasion the Romans had constructed elaborate wooden siege-works which they managed to move right up to the walls of Veii, but before they could use them to launch a major attack, the Veientanes opened their gates and ran out with firebrands to set the whole structure on fire. In a few minutes the work of months was left a smouldering heap of ashes.

Disasters like this made the Romans more and more depressed. It looked as if the war would never end, and there was much unrest as taxes were increased and conscription became even more severe. Farms and industries were emptied of men who were sent off to spend the best years of their lives in the firing line. And the position was made even worse by a series of hard winters followed by bad summers in which every kind of disease was rife. The priests tried to find some way of improving the situation by introducing new religious ceremonies but they seemed to be of little use and morale sank to an even lower level as the army was defeated in one engagement after another.

Just at this moment a very curious event was reported which the Romans at once took to be a sign from heaven though no one was able to explain exactly what it meant. The summer had been hot and dry with only occasional showers but suddenly for no apparent reason the level of a lake in the centre of the Alban hills, about twenty miles from Rome, began to rise. It got higher and higher until the Romans decided to send a delegation to the great Greek oracle at Delphi to enquire what they should do about it. Before they could get a reply from there, someone nearer at hand gave them the clue. The Roman and Veientane lines at this time were so close together that the troops used to talk to one another from the trenches. One day, an old man, who had a reputation as a soothsayer, came wandering along the Veientane lines and as he walked he kept muttering to himself 'if the water falls, Veii will fall'. The Roman soldiers overheard this and at first they just laughed at him as a silly old man but when they learnt from casual conversation that he was supposed to be a soothsayer and to have the gift of

Lake Albano today

second sight, they took it more seriously. One of the Roman sentries accosted him on the pretence that he wanted to consult him on some private matter of his own. He invited him over to the Roman lines and then in full view of the Veientanes seized him by the arm and marched him off to headquarters. The Roman general at once sent him under escort to Rome. The old man accepted his fate philosophically and agreed to tell everything that he knew because it was plain to him that this was what the gods wanted and that there was no point trying to conceal it. There was, he explained, a very old Etruscan prophecy that Veii could never be captured until the waters of the Alban lake were drained, and this was what he had been repeating to himself when he was overheard. The Romans, however, were suspicious. The story sounded thin and, in any case, it would be a tremendous engineering feat to drain the lake. So they decided to wait until their delegates returned from Delphi. The reply which they eventually brought back from Greece corresponded exactly with what the old man had said. The Romans were recommended to drain the Alban lake if they wanted to end the long and costly war.

An underground tunnel at Veii

The Senate decided to act on this advice. They constructed a long tunnel as an overflow from the lake to regulate its level and in the confidence that the war was reaching its climax they appointed M. Furius Camillus dictator with P. Cornelius Scipio as his adjutant. The change in command had a dramatic effect. Hopes began to rise and there was soon a new spirit in the ranks, which Camillus encouraged by taking firm measures to restore discipline among the troops. Volunteers poured in from all Rome's allies to join the army so that before long he was in a position of clear superiority, and he improved it by forbidding the small engagements which in the past had proved so costly to the Romans. Instead he employed the men in digging a great mine or tunnel underneath the walls of Veii which was to come up in the centre of the enemy stronghold. It was a huge operation and to keep it going night and day he divided the men into six shifts which took it in turns to dig. Eventually it was almost finished and Camillus gave instructions for the final attack. First of all he prayed to the two gods who were most concerned with the fate of Veii. He offered to give Apollo of Delphi a tenth of all the loot if they were successful, because he had given them the original prophecy. He also promised Juno, who was the protecting goddess of Veii, that he would build her a wonderful new temple at Rome if she would help the Romans instead of the Veientanes. Then he ordered his troops to attack the walls of the city from every point of the compass. The Veientanes were surprised at this sudden activity after so long a lull and they were confident that they could repel the attacks as they had often done before. But in fact it was all a trick, because while the enemy's attention was distracted by the fierce fire against the walls, a picked body of storm-troopers emerged from the mine into the very heart of the city and attacked the defenders in the rear. In a second everything was thrown into chaos. Despite the desperate attempts of women and slaves to stop them by throwing stones and tiles from the roofs of the houses, they were able to set fire to several parts of the city and to force open one of the main gates. This let the rest of the Romans in and before long the whole city was overrun. There was nearly a complete massacre before Camillus was able to enforce a cease-fire but in the end the Veientanes surrendered and their lives were spared.

The problem that now faced Camillus was what to do with all the loot. Veii was a very rich city and there were thousands of prisoners who would be sold into slavery. The choice seemed to lie between allowing the soldiers to take whatever they could lay their hands on and commandeering it all for the Roman treasury. Either way was likely to make Camillus unpopular because there were bound to be squabbles and complaints. So he had referred the question to the Senate who after some discussion decided that the troops should be rewarded by being allowed to loot at will. But when Camillus realized the full extent of the wealth which was at their mercy, he was even more alarmed. Although he took great care to reserve a tenth of it for Apollo, as he had promised, he prayed that the other gods would not be jealous at the success of the Romans. But, as he prayed, he slipped and fell, and this was afterwards taken

Apollo of Veii

to be an omen: for within a few years Camillus was exiled and Rome herself was captured by the Gauls.

For the moment, however, all was joy and celebration. The soldiers roamed through the streets picking up everything that they could see until there was nothing of any value left in Veii. Only one thing now remained to be done. Camillus had promised to give Juno a new home. So he selected some men to carry her statue to Rome. They washed and dressed themselves in white robes specially for this duty but when they entered the temple they were nervous about actually touching such a holy statue and hesitated until they saw the goddess appear to nod to them. Then they believed that she wanted to leave Veii and certainly they had no difficulty in lifting and carrying the statue safely to Rome where Camillus built a temple for her on the Aventine Hill.

That was the end of Veii—one of the richest Etruscan cities of her time.

The Faliscan Schoolmaster

The capture of Veii had to be rounded off by defeating Falerii, a town nearby which had loyally supported Veii during the war. Once again, Camillus was appointed general of the Roman army. He began the campaign energetically, by burning their crops and ransacking their farms, but the town of Falerii itself was difficult to capture since it was on a rocky hill surrounded by steep precipices. It was too strong to be attacked openly and the only hope was to starve it into surrender. So Camillus and his army settled down to wait and, since Falerii was well-supplied with food, they might have had to wait another ten years but for a strange piece of luck. The chief citizens of Falerii employed a tutor to look after their sons, who taught them their lessons and also supervised their games. He used to take the boys everyday for a walk in the country and he continued to do so even after war had been declared. Sometimes they went only a short way from the town, sometimes they made longer expeditions until one day they found that he had led them right into the Roman camp and handed them over as hostages to Camillus, in the hope of making some money for himself. Camillus, however, refused to have anything to do with such un-Roman treachery: war had its rules just as much as peace and the Romans had no quarrel with innocent children who were not to blame for what their parents had done. So he made the schoolmaster take off his clothes, tied his hands behind his back and gave the boys sticks to beat him all the way home. The Faliscans watched this unusual sight and then considered what steps they ought to take. Up till now they had been full of defiance and hate against the Romans but now they were so overwhelmed by the humanity and justice which Camillus had shown that they decided unanimously to stop the war. They sent a delegation to Camillus who gave them a safe-conduct to Rome. When they reached Rome, they were introduced into the Senate and offered the unconditional surrender of their city in a short speech. 'You have won a great moral victory, Romans, over us and have convinced us that we should be better off under your system of government than under our own. You have shown the world that honesty is more important than success.'

The Capture of Rome

The Romans were always fighting with invaders, mostly from the north. There were many bitter battles and much blood shed. But they never thought that the city of Rome itself was in danger. Yet it was once captured by the Gauls and the whole future of Roman power was threatened. It happened in this way.

The Gauls were already established in the northern parts of Italy but they had never succeeded in getting a firm hold on the Appennines. The actual attack of the Gauls on Rome is said to have been the result of an accident. Rome sent ambassadors to warn the Gauls against attacking the city of Clusium. These ambassadors so far forgot their duty as diplomats as to fight against the Gauls. The Roman people, instead of punishing them for their misconduct, elected them military tribunes for the next year. Because of this, the Gauls were furious. They diverted their attack from Clusium to Rome and poured southwards down the left bank of the Tiber. Their wild songs and savage yells filled the air with hideous noise. The Romans were completely taken by surprise. They had never before encountered the onrush of the northern barbarians. The Roman army drawn up on the banks of the Allia, only eleven miles from Rome, was completely defeated and scattered. The city was left without defence.

Now, in this great emergency, the real greatness of Rome appears. While many of the fugitives from the Roman army fled to the city of Veii, the Capitol in Rome was occupied by a strong force of Roman soldiers. The senators also took refuge there and the holy treasures were removed and buried. Thus, in spite of the capture of the city, the government and religion of Rome survived. The story is told of how the vestal virgins carried their precious relics, sharing the burden, along the road to the citadel. As they struggled up the hill, a working man called Lucius Albinus overtook them with the farm-waggon in which he was evacuating his wife and children. Seeing the plight of the virgins, he ordered his family to get down from the cart and carried the girls and their relics to safety.

The Gauls were staggered by their success. They rushed through the streets of Rome looking for booty. They found the houses of the nobles, near the Forum, open and the nobles themselves sitting silent and motionless in their halls, dressed in all their most splendid robes. To the astonished Gauls they appeared to be not men but gods. One Gaul dared to stroke the beard of one of the nobles called Marcus Papirius. This nobleman, in anger, struck him over the head with an ivory cane. The Gaul, finding his god human after all, killed him, and the massacre of all the other nobles followed.

Meanwhile the Romans in the Capitol looked down upon their tragic city ruined by fire and sword. But their courage never left them and they resolved to defend the citadel to the death. One young Roman, Gaius Fabius Dorsuo, even passed through the enemy lines unharmed. He was determined to go to the family burying place on the Quirinal Hill, now held by the Gauls. Every year a service of remembrance was held there for his ancestors and Gaius, holding the sacred vessels necessary for this service, went there and back unmolested by the Gauls who were astonished at his nerve.

Only once was the citadel in grave danger in spite of many attacks by the enemy. This was when a young Roman called Pontius Cominus, one of the survivors of the Roman army at Veii, floated down the Tiber on a strip of cork. He brought with him a request to the Senate to recall brave Camillus from exile to lead the new army. He climbed to the citadel by an easy ascent, so far unnoticed by either the Gauls or the Romans. Having accomplished his mission he returned the same way.

But the Gauls had marked his route. On a star-lit night a party of them clambered, one by one, to the very top of the hill. They escaped detection because the guard on that part of the defences had fallen asleep on duty. Fortunately the holy geese who lived on the citadel had not been killed in spite of a great shortage of food. These birds by their cackling and gabbling and flapping of wings woke the consul Marcus Manlius. Snatching his weapons he strode past his bewildered comrades and struck a Gaul, who had already obtained a foothold on the crest of the hill, with the boss of his shield. This Gaul slipped and fell upon the others who were climbing up the rocks behind him. All were repulsed with confusion and loss. Manlius had saved the day and his comrades honoured him. Each brought him a small offering of bread and wine out of his own meagre rations as a token of their gratitude. The sentinel who had been asleep was thrown from the rock.

Both Romans and Gauls were now suffering badly from want of provisions and disease. The Romans, indeed, tossed precious hunks of bread to the Gauls to pretend they were not starving but they were near despair. A truce was at last arranged and the Gauls declared they would be prepared to withdraw from the city if the Romans paid them a very large ransom in gold.

But help was at hand. Camillus was now in command of the Roman army in exile and marched on the city. He arrived in the very nick of time. The Gauls were actually weighing out the gold which was to be the price of their withdrawal from Rome. Camillus himself saw Brennus, the leader of the Gauls, throw his sword into the scale with the humiliating words 'winner takes all'. That was the last straw for the Romans. Camillus turned upon the Gauls, tore up the peace treaty and drove the enemy out of Rome. He also recovered all the gold which had been paid over to the enemy.

Rome was saved but it was only a shambles. Blood, toil, tears and sweat were needed to rebuild it. A proud new city arose from the ruins and the Roman people valued their freedom as they had never done before.

The Fall of Manlius

It is sad to have to tell how Manlius who had been so brave in defending the Capitol, was corrupted by his popularity. He became very jealous of Camillus, a brilliant soldier, who bore the brunt of the fighting when the Gauls were eventually driven back from Rome. Manlius knew he had lost favour with the nobles and this brought out all the worst in his character. He set about, in all sorts of ways, to curry favour with the common people.

Meanwhile Camillus was chosen dictator although he still had to spend most of his time with the army in the field. One day, however, he was summoned back to Rome to deal with trouble which was being stirred up by the disgruntled Manlius. Things reached a climax when an officer who had done well in the war got into trouble with the moneylenders and was sent to prison for debt. Manlius saw him being led off and sprang to his defence. He made an impassioned speech in the Forum contrasting the plight of the unfortunate officer with the nobles who stayed at home and feathered their nests while the army was at war. His audience were sympathetic to him, especially when he himself paid the officer's debts and set him free. He also publicly sold one of his farms, giving the money to help ex-soldiers who found themselves in difficulties.

Not content with the popularity he gained with these acts Manlius now made his house a centre for spreading sedition among the citizens. He constantly accused the nobles with having appropriated the gold actually paid to the Gauls as ransom money. Naturally the Romans were annoyed as this money had originally come out of their own pockets. It was at this point that the government became anxious and recalled Camillus.

He at once challenged Manlius to prove the truth of his story by giving the names of the men who had obtained secret hoards of public gold. If he failed to make his case, he would be guilty of plotting against the state and must face the death penalty.

In spite of impassioned speeches about bad government Manlius could not produce the necessary evidence. He was thrown into prison on a charge of spreading untrue rumours against the state. He still, however, had his supporters who stood about the prison gates unwashed and with uncut hair and beards as a sign of mourning for their lost leader. There was also much grumbling and discontent by the ex-soldiers who considered their pensions and grants of land inadequate. Manlius languished in gaol but his popularity with the common people continued to grow. They told, and re-told, the story of how he had, single-handed, hurled down the Gauls who were storming the Tarpeian Rock. Plots were made to storm the prison and rescue him. The Senate suddenly panicked and released him. The result was inevitable. Manlius was now the acknowledged leader of the discontented mob and he became more and more irresponsible.

The Senate were well aware of the danger, but they were anxious to make it a personal quarrel between Manlius and Camillus, and were prepared to overlook the discontent of his followers. The last thing they wanted was civil war. They summoned Manlius to meet them and defend his case. Manlius spoke with all his usual eloquence and passion. He used all the dramatic effects of which he was a master. He bared his breast to show the scars of his war-wounds. He pointed to the Capitol, the scene of his finest hour, and called on the ancient gods to come to his defence.

To the Senate all this was intolerable. They could see the effect that Manlius was having on the crowd and that the situation was hourly becoming more dangerous. They therefore decided to remove the place of the trial from the centre of the city to a wood outside the city, and well out of view of the Capitol. There they charged Manlius with treason and condemned him to death. Before the news could reach his supporters they carried him up to the top of the Capitol and flung him from the Tarpeian Rock.

The Romans were horror-struck by his end. It was not only the cruel manner of it, but the tragic irony that the same spot marked the place of his greatest triumph and his infamous death. The riot was calmed but the Senate were still determined to take no risks. The family of the wretched Manlius were banished for ever from the Capitol and none of his clan in future could bear the name of Marcus. For traitors there could be no mercy under Roman rule.

But that was not the end of the Gauls. Groups of them continued to drift down from the north of Italy and harassed Rome and the surrounding countryside. They did not often dare to face the Romans in pitched battle (and, when they did, they were usually defeated) but they took to the hills and carried on a constant guerilla warfare, threatening Rome's communications and damaging her trade. For the next fifty years, until about 340 B.C. Rome was never free from this thorn in her flesh. Livy tells two of the exciting incidents which happened during that period.

On one occasion the Gauls had mobilised a large force and had marched to a point some three miles north of the city, where there was a crossing over the river. The Romans were thrown into confusion at their approach. They proclaimed a state of emergency, called up every able-bodied man and hurried along the river-bank to defend the crossing. So the two armies lay encamped on opposite banks with the bridge in between, and the situation seemed a deadlock with neither side able to move until a giant Gaul strode on to the deserted bridge and challenged any Roman to come out and fight him in single combat. For a long time not a single Roman volunteered: the odds looked too heavily against them. Then a young private, Lucius Manlius, stepped from the ranks and, approaching the general, Quinctius Poenus, asked permission to speak. 'I would not presume, Sir, to exceed my rank and I'm well aware of the risks. But if you let me, I will show that brute over there that I come from a family that knows how to deal with Gauls.' Poenus readily gave his consent and wished him the very best of luck. Manlius then armed himself carefully, choosing a small, round shield and a short, pointed sword which was useful for close fighting. So equipped he went out to meet the Gaul, while the two armies stood by with mixed feelings to watch this unevenly matched duel. On the one side was the enormous Gaul, singing and dancing and sticking his tongue out, dressed in a brilliantly-coloured tunic and golden armour: on the other was a squat, ordinary Roman soldier who betrayed by his manner and expression none of the feelings inside him. The Gaul began the fight by a slashing sword-stroke. Manlius parried it with his shield and then, before the Gaul could recover his balance, he knocked his guard aside with the edge of his shield and, closing with him, gave two quick jabs at his stomach. The giant tumbled to the ground and lay there stretched out flat. It was all over in a minute. Manlius did not mutilate the body but simply removed the golden chain or torque which the Gaul had worn round his neck, and put it on his own. The Romans gave him a hero's welcome while the Gauls were stunned with surprise and alarm. That is how he earned the surname Torquatus which was handed down for many generations in the Manlian family.

 The second incident, which was even more remarkable, took place a few years later, when L. Furius Camillus, the son of the great Camillus, was consul. The Gauls at this time were skulking in the hills around Rome, but the bitterly cold winter weather at last forced them down into the wide plains south of Rome which stretched between the mountains and the sea. At once they began to loot everything that they could lay their hands on and at the same

A Gallic warrior

time a fleet of Greek pirates descended on the coast and caused a lot of damage there too, until the whole countryside became too dangerous to live in. The news of these troubles made the Romans take the offensive and they sent Camillus with an army to police the area. He hoped to avoid having to fight an actual battle since his troops were raw recruits but believed that their presence would be enough to keep the peace. One day while the soldiers were quietly attending to their guard duties a tall, well-armed Gaul marched up to the headquarters of the Roman army and, obtaining silence by beating his spear on his shield, challenged any Roman to dare to come out and fight him. Among the Roman officers there was a young subaltern, called Marcus Valerius, who remembered the story about Manlius and thought himself quite as brave. So, after

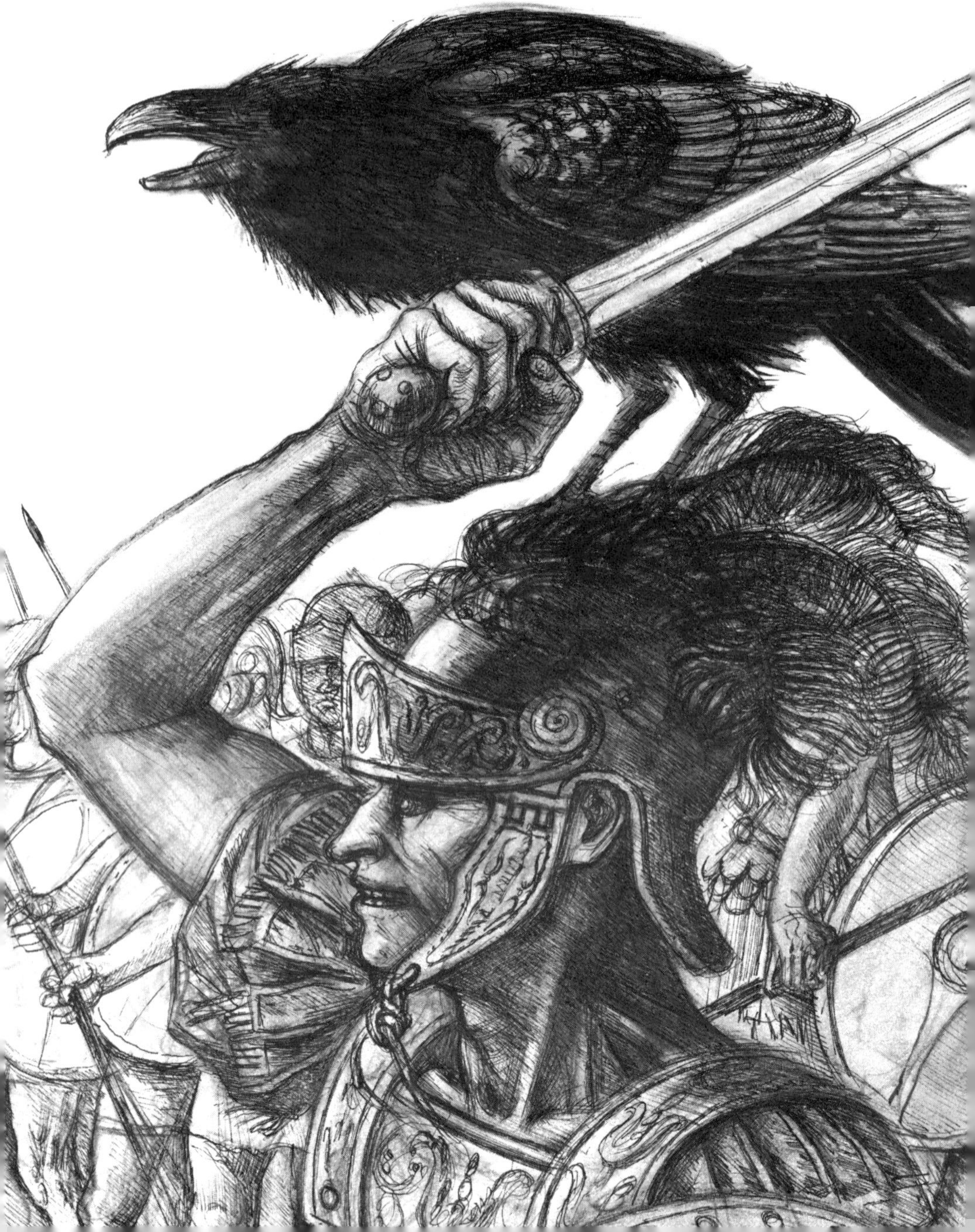

getting his general's permission, he accepted the challenge and went to face the Gaul. Everyone was on tenterhooks as they watched the two men. Old memories revived, as history seemed to be repeating itself, but suddenly there was a dramatic intervention. A great, black raven flew down and settled on Valerius' helmet. Valerius welcomed the strange arrival of the bird as a good sign and so it proved to be. Every time Valerius and the Gaul came to grips, the raven stretched its wings and savagely attacked the Gaul's face with its claws and beak. This upset his aim and panicked him so that Valerius was able to catch him off his guard and kill him with a single blow. A stunned silence fell on both sides, for they felt that the gods must have had a hand in what had happened, but when Valerius began to remove his opponent's armour, the other Gauls were roused to action. But it was too late. The Romans were so excited by Valerius' success that they rushed forward and drove the Gauls from the field, and did not stop until they had chased them for good right out of that part of the country. This exploit also earned Valerius, like Manlius, a new surname—Corvinus or 'Raven'.

The Son of Manlius Torquatus

In war discipline is essential. It has been proved over and over again that sheer size can actually be a handicap if it is not properly controlled. The Crusaders were a handful of men compared with the Saracen hordes but their superior training outweighed their numerical weakness. Nearly 2,000 years before that the same point had been made by the Greeks who, although greatly outnumbered, had no difficulty in defeating the ill-disciplined rabble of the Persians on the plain of Plataea. So it is not surprising that the Romans attached great importance to unquestioning obedience in the field. Sometimes this stern sense of duty could lead to tragic consequences as it did in the case of Manlius Torquatus. Manlius, it will be remembered, had earned his surname by his courage in killing a giant Gaul single-handed and removing the necklace from round his neck. He was now older, with a son of his own of military age, and he had become one of the most respected leaders at Rome.

During one of the numerous campaigns against the Samnites, the young Manlius was in charge of a small party of cavalry who had been sent forward to reconnoitre the ground in front of the main army. They had strict instructions not to get involved in any fighting. Quite unexpectedly they stumbled upon the main base of enemy operations which was in charge of a man called Maecius the Twin, a Latin from the town of Tusculum some thirty miles from Rome. Manlius rode up to just out of range of the camp and examined it closely. As he did so, Maecius taunted him and dared him to fight. Manlius, remembering his instructions, contented himself with replying that Maecius would have to fight for his life all too soon when the main Roman army caught up with him. Maecius then accused him of cowardice: 'You wouldn't even dare to face me man to man, would you?' he jeered. 'You are scared of finding out how much better Tusculans are than Romans'.

This was too much for Manlius. He had always been a hot-headed boy and now these taunts stung him to the quick. He forgot all about his father's instructions; he forgot all about the mission on which he had been sent. All he cared about was to lay hands on this impertinent foreigner. He didn't even care whether he won or lost so long as he could have the satisfaction of having a go at him. The two men dug their spurs into their horses' flanks and charged at each other. On the first attempt both missed, but they wheeled round and galloped to the attack again. This time Manlius' lance pierced the ear of Maecius' horse which reared up in pain and threw its rider. Maecius was now at Manlius' mercy and to strike him down and remove his armour was the work of an instant.

But when Manlius returned to headquarters highly pleased with himself and his exploit, his father took a very different view. 'Orders are orders', he said, 'and you have deliberately flouted the specific instructions which I gave you. If this kind of thing were to spread, it would be the end of the Roman army. I am sorry that it should be my son, of all people, who should do such a thing but this fact will not stop me from doing my duty'. Thereupon he told an orderly to bind him to a stake and with a single blow of an axe he cut off his head.

The soldiers were appalled at such ruthless punishment but the lesson was a salutary one for it tightened up the discipline throughout the army.

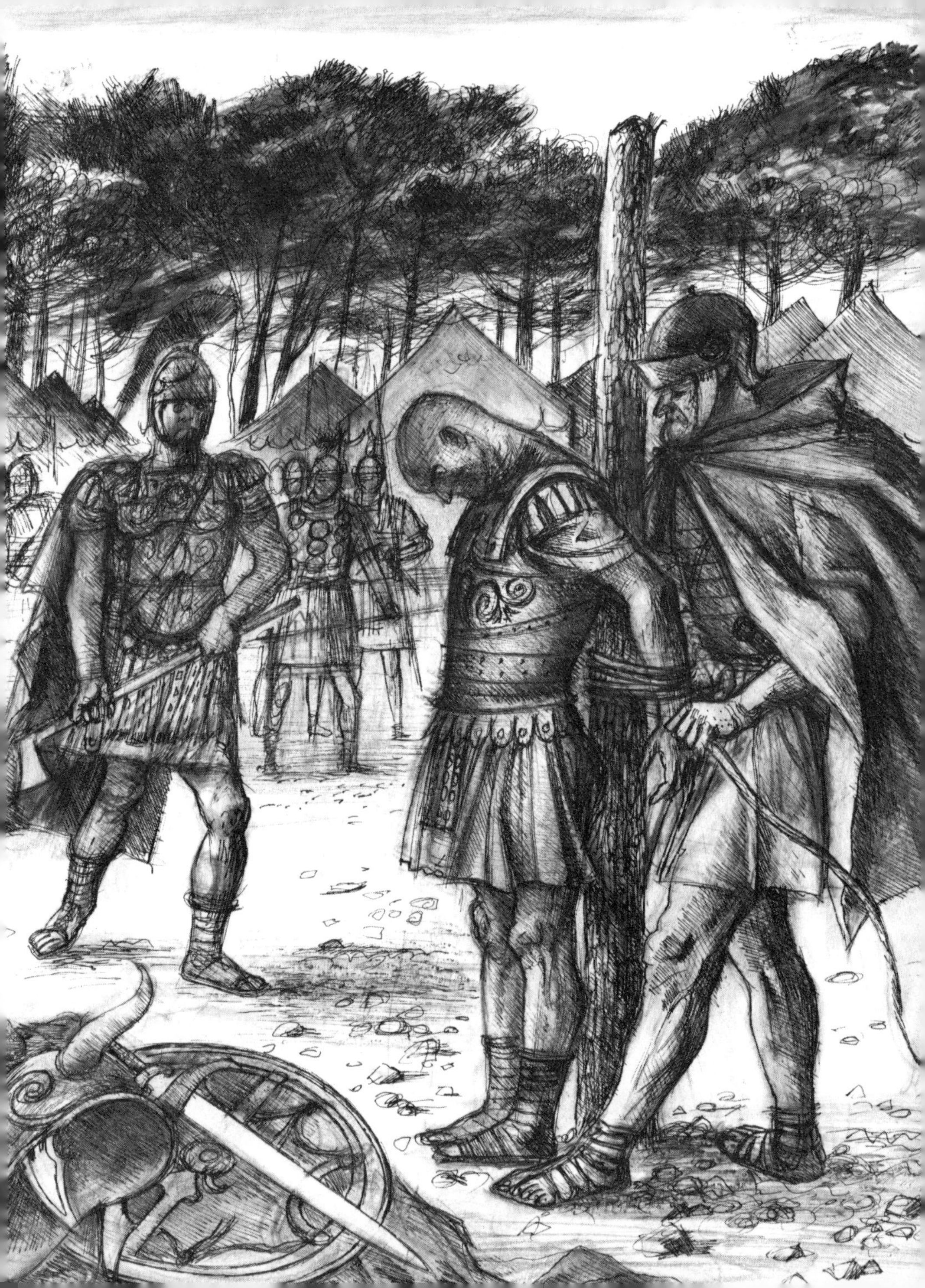

The Caudine Forks

By such victories the Romans at last began to master the Gauls and there is no doubt that they would have driven them out of Italy and back over the Alps to their own country if the Gauls had not made friends with a powerful nation, the Samnites, who lived in the south of Italy. The Samnites declared war on the Romans in 343 B.C. and the war dragged on for more than fifty years. At times the Romans were very hard pressed, since they were forced to fight on two fronts at once, against the Gauls and against the Samnites. The blackest moment came in the year 321 B.C. when the Roman army suffered the worst humiliation in its history.

The Samnites had been discussing with Rome the possibility of reaching an agreement to end the war. Both sides were tired of fighting and had suffered heavy casualties; so it seemed that if they could get round a table and talk it over, they would be able to negotiate a fair peace. The Samnites in particular had gone out of their way to make concessions in the hope that these would soften Roman resistance. They had returned all the property that had been captured in the course of the war. They had executed various ring-leaders who had stirred up anti-Roman demonstrations and had handed their bodies over to the Romans. But these gestures had failed to impress the Romans who continued to behave in an obstinate and aggressive way, insisting that they would be satisfied with nothing less than unconditional surrender.

This was a stupid attitude for the Romans to adopt, because it drove the Samnites to bitter opposition. They felt that they had right on their side and were fighting for a just cause, since they had been willing to agree to arbitration whereas the Romans would only be content with blood. And people fight all the harder and all the better when they are convinced that they are in the right and are under the protection of heaven.

A Samnite warrior

So the Samnites mobilized their army and prepared for war. Their plan, which was designed to mislead and fool the Romans, was very clever. The Roman army was at a place called Calatia, where it was securely stationed. As there was no future in launching a direct attack on it there, the Samnite general, Pontius, had the bright idea of inducing them to leave their safe defences by making them believe that the Samnite army was many miles away in Apulia and was on the point of capturing the vital town of Luceria, which was allied to Rome. To do this he dressed up a dozen soldiers as shepherds and sent them out to graze their flocks within earshot of the Roman sentries. The Romans overheard them as they gossipped about what was happening at Luceria and the rumour seemed to be confirmed by the accounts which were given by stray prisoners-of-war.

The news thoroughly alarmed the Romans. Not only was Luceria a loyal ally but there was a serious danger that if Luceria fell the whole of Apulia would desert to the Samnites. At all costs, Luceria must be saved. The Romans, therefore, decided to march post-haste to its relief. But in fact the Samnite army was nowhere near Luceria; it was in hiding not far from the Roman camp, watching which route the Romans would take. For there was a difficult choice. They could either go by the long but safe coast road to Apulia or they could risk the much shorter route through the hills by way of a valley known as the Caudine Forks. After some discussion, they decided that time was of the essence and that they should choose the shorter route. When the Samnites saw which way they were going, they quietly made their plans and took up their positions.

The Caudine Forks is a curious piece of ground. A narrow valley, surrounded on both sides by high, wooded mountains, leads into a large round basin which is ringed by hills. At the other side of the basin another defile, even steeper and narrower than the first, leads down to the plains of Apulia. The basin itself, which the road goes straight across, is an attractive plain with lush grass and pleasant streams. The Romans had no difficulty making their way into it but when they reached the defile at the far end they found that it had been blocked by rocks and tree-trunks so that they could not force their way out. They turned round, therefore, and tried to get out by the way that they had come but it was too late. That exit also was now blocked, and the hill-tops all round were stiff with enemy soldiers. The Romans realized that they were trapped; there was no hope of escape. For a moment or two they stood stock still, overwhelmed by despair, but then their old discipline and habit reasserted itself and they pathetically began to pitch camp. No one had the heart to give orders: it was just an automatic reaction to unload their spades and picks and start digging.

At last, as night fell, they had fortified some kind of a camp. As they sat there gloomily cooking their dinner and listening to the hoots of derision from the enemy all round, they argued what

Samniums and the Caudine. Forks

to do next. Some were for making a desperate attack on the Samnites, even if it meant storming the rocky heights around them and even if it were to end in glorious failure. Others felt that there was no point in further action, they were caught, that was all there was to it. So they argued into the night. But the Samnites also were so taken aback by their own success that they couln't decide on the next move.

In the end they referred the problem to Pontius' aged father who had been their leader in previous wars. His first advice was to let the Romans go unharmed. This did not appeal to them at all, so they consulted him again. This time he advised them to kill every single Roman to the last man. This advice was so much at variance with what he had suggested earlier that Pontius had to admit that his father must have become senile. But so great was their respect for the old man that they agreed to fetch him so that he could explain in person what was the point of his puzzling advice. When he arrived in a farm-waggon at the Samnite camp, he defended his two opinions by saying that if they followed his first advice, their unexpected kindness would so impress the Romans that a lasting peace could easily be concluded whereas his second advice would at least ensure that the Romans would be too weak to attack them for years to come. After further discussion, however, they reached a compromise, to release the Romans but to do so after having subjected them to all the humiliations of defeat. Pontius' father complained that this would get the worst of both worlds, since the Romans would neither be weakened nor conciliated, but they did not listen to him. So when the Romans were finally driven by hunger and exhaustion to ask for a truce, Pontius told them that his terms were simple: they were to hand over their arms and equipment and clothes: he would make them walk under a yoke, to demonstrate publicly that they were no better than slaves, and then, in just their shirts, they were to leave the country for ever. These terms appalled the Romans. Even the generals were too flabbergasted to speak, until one of the staff-officers, L. Lentulus, whose father had been the only senator to oppose the motion that the Gauls should be bought off with gold when they had captured Rome sixty years before, proposed that they should accept Pontius' terms. He argued that they really had no option, for without the army the city of Rome would no longer be able to exist. If they saved the army, they would at least live to fight another day whereas it was futile to stand on their dignity. Reluctantly the generals agreed and told Pontius that they accepted his terms for the release of the army but that a treaty to settle the future relations between Rome and Samnium could only be authorised by the Senate. They had no power to commit the Roman people but they were prepared to leave 100 hostages with the Samnites until a satisfactory peace was made.

This was the best bargain that the Romans could make and it filled the ordinary decent soldier with shame to think how he had been led by the incompetence of his generals into a trap, like a wild animal, and how he could only escape by being made a laughingstock in the eyes of the world. They had lost the battle, they had lost the war, they had lost everything without even having had the chance of striking a blow in their own defence. And their eyes filled with tears as they marched out of the camp and watched their generals being stripped of their uniform and made to walk, barefoot and half-naked, under a yoke held over them. Then it was the turn of each battalion to suffer the same indignity while their enemies jeered at them and poked them with swords. Eventually it was all over; the whole army was free again, but they had nothing other than the shirts on their backs.

They shambled away towards Capua, disorganized and utterly dispirited. Indeed they were so ashamed of themselves that they did not dare enter Capua itself but halted a few miles outside. Their allies, however, showed great sympathy and understanding in their embarrassment. Without asking questions, they brought supplies of clothing and arms, provided horses and transport and offered them every hospitality.

So ended a sorry episode in the history of the Roman army. The Senate afterwards disavowed the decision of the generals to yield to Pontius' terms and later campaigns went some way towards restoring Roman pride and prestige.

The Death of P. Decius

The decisive battle in the war against the Samnites and the Gauls was fought in 295 B.C. near the town of Sentinum in Umbria. On this occasion the enemy army was reinforced by detachments from other nations so that the Romans were greatly outnumbered but they had two outstanding generals, Q. Fabius and P. Decius, who were great friends and had served together for many years. There was, therefore, no disagreement on the Roman side about how the war should be fought whereas the opposing generals were perpetually squabbling about their objectives and language difficulties (some spoke Etruscan, some Celtic, some Samnite) made the misunderstandings even worse. However, they had agreed to unite for a rapid thrust at Rome itself and for this purpose they had crossed the Apennines and were moving through Umbria. The Romans, sizing up the situation, decided to block their advance at Sentinum and had hurriedly assembled an army of four divisions with a large force of cavalry.

The two armies took up their positions but in the lull before zero hour, as they waited for the battle to begin, they saw a

remarkable sight. A deer came running between the lines, chased down from the mountains by a wolf. Half way along the deer swerved and headed towards the Gauls who promptly shot it, while the wolf made for the Roman front line. The Roman ranks parted and let it pass through unscathed. One of the soldiers who watched this strange event predicted that it meant that the Gauls would run away and be killed whereas the Romans, whose ancestors had been nursed by a wolf, would emerge unharmed from the battle. But the battle was not in fact as simple as that. Fabius, who had command of the right wing, reckoned that his best policy was to stand on the defensive until the first fury of the Gauls and Samnites had exhausted itself; for the Samnites were easily discouraged and the physique of the Gauls was not adapted to enduring excessive heat and effort. So he ordered his men not to take the offensive until he gave them the word but to beat off any attacks that were made on them. Decius, on the other hand, who led the left wing, was much more impetuous. He liked action, the more violent and dangerous the better. Impatient with the slow progress that the infantry seemed to be making, he decided to bring his cavalry into action in order to speed things up. As it turned out this was a rash step to take. For, although he won two quick skirmishes, he was suddenly caught off balance by the armoured chariots which the Gauls had been keeping in reserve and which they now suddenly launched in a furious charge at him. These chariots unnerved the Romans, and scared their horses which were not used to the din. Decius fell back in confusion on his own infantry, thereby throwing them into disorder too. The situation was now in danger of getting out of hand, for the infantry and cavalry were hopelessly muddled and the Gauls had only to press home their attack and the whole Roman army would be destroyed. But at this crisis Decius remembered something which his father had done many years before. Recognising that it was his own fault and determined, if he could, to atone for it himself and so appease the displeasure of the gods, he got M. Livius, the priest, who was in attendance on him, to pronounce the solemn formula of dedication, by which he gave up his own life to the powers of earth and darkness in order that the Romans might be saved. Then he prayed that the curse which had fallen on him should be transferred to his enemies and that his death should paralyse and blight their power. Having spoken this prayer he rode into the thickest part of the fight and was instantly killed.

His death had a wonderful effect on Roman morale. When they had recovered from their immediate shock, the soldiers re-formed and returned to the attack. They seemed to be inspired with a superhuman energy which made them irresistible as they drove through the massed rows of Gallic shields. On the other wing, Fabius had heard of Decius' brave gesture and had seen the dramatic change in Roman fortunes. His instinct told him that the moment had come to move from defence to attack and he gave the signal to advance.

The whole line surged forward, sweeping the Samnites from the field and storming their base camp.

The victory was total and complete. But the Roman casualties were not light. Over 8,000 men had been killed and, in addition, one of their most successful generals whom they could ill afford to lose. It took them two days to find his body and, when they did, they gave him a ceremonial burial, with full military honours.

Crossing the Alps

As Rome became a great empire, she came into contact with other powerful cities across the sea. One of her most dangerous rivals and enemies was the city of Carthage in North Africa. Carthage was a commercial state which traded all over the Mediterranean. She had colonies in Sicily and in Spain and watched jealously as Rome began to encroach on her territories until at last she decided that she must resist Roman expansion. The first war between Rome and Carthage was indecisive; neither side could really claim victory. During the peace which followed both countries tried to improve their position because they felt that another war was inevitable. In the end it was Carthage which triggered it off by attacking Saguntum, a city in Spain which was an ally of Rome. The Carthaginian general Hannibal saw that his best chance was to act very quickly before the Romans were properly mobilized. So he decided on the daring step of invading Italy with his army. To do this he had to cross the Alps which block the way between France and Italy. It was an astonishing adventure.

Hannibal's soldiers were scared at the prospect. They had heard terrifying stories about the ice and the snow and the wild beasts of the Alps. But Hannibal reassured them by reminding them that the Alps had been crossed by an army before—by the Gauls who had conquered Rome 200 years ago—and that they had faced much greater dangers and difficulties already. So far from touching the sky, the mountains were not really all that high since people lived in them and farmed there. He urged them not to allow such a minor obstacle to prevent them from reaching their main objective which was Rome. The troops were somewhat calmed by Hannibal's

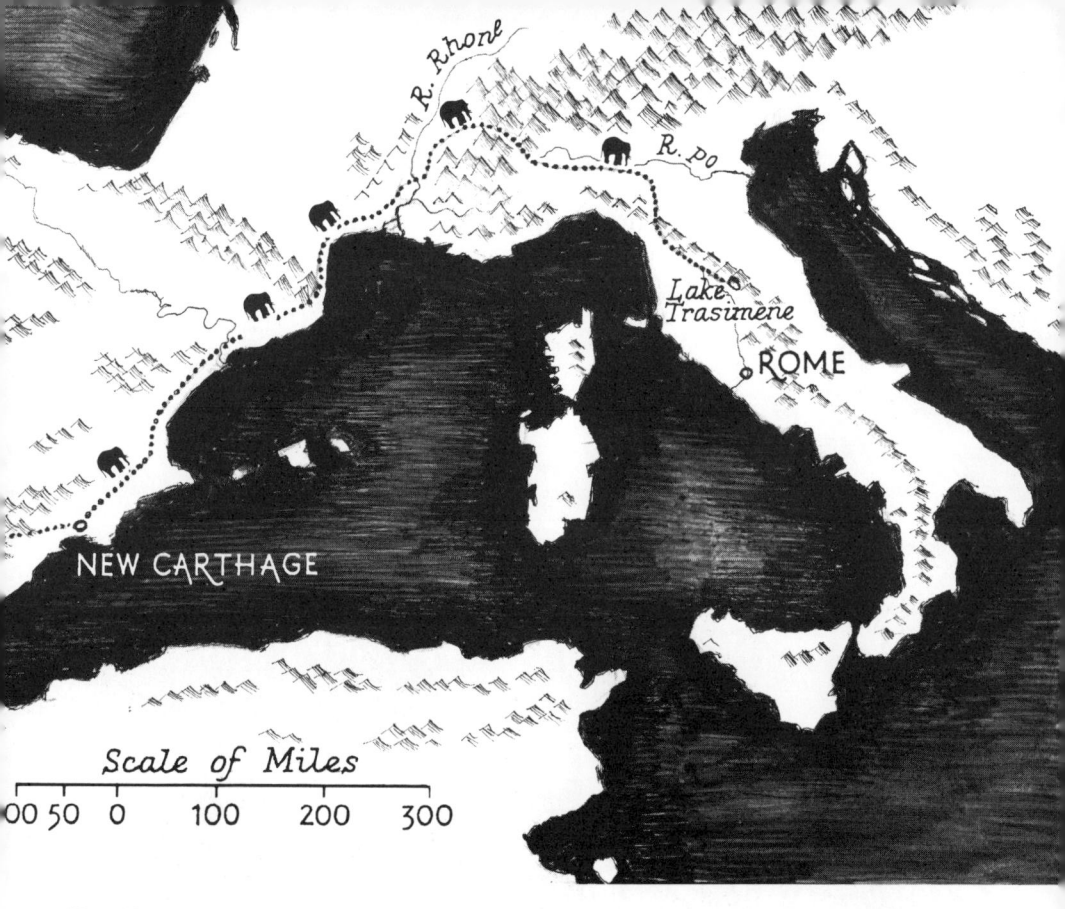

Hannibal's route

arguments, particularly since they knew that Italy lay just the other side of the Alps and that it would be a waste of effort to give up within sight of their goal. So after a day's rest, they started off, travelling north along the Rhone valley towards central Gaul. It was not the most direct way but Hannibal chose it because the further they were from the coast the less likely they were to meet a Roman army and Hannibal did not want to fight until he reached Italy. Four days later he came to the junction of the rivers Isaras and Rhone which flow down from the Alps and enclose a piece of land known as the Island. Here after some delicate negotiations he succeeded in gaining the support of a powerful local tribe, the

Allobroges, who in return gave him supplies and clothes which he badly needed for facing the notorious cold of the high Alps.

He was now ready for the main ascent. For a while he continued in a northerly direction until he reached the Druentia. This is a very tricky river to cross, since the bottom is too treacherous to afford a safe footing and the current is so fast that it is impossible to float rafts or boats on it. On this occasion it was in spate after some recent heavy rains which had brought down a lot of stones and gravel. But eventually after a good deal of panic and chaos in which some lives and much equipment were lost, Hannibal managed to get his army over to the other side.

They now made their way unopposed across open country to the foothills of the Alps. Here they were able to see for the first time what they had only heard about before—the towering peaks, the snowclad pinnacles soaring to the sky, the animals shrivelled with cold, the wild and ragged shepherds. All these sights increased their fear, particularly as they tackled the first slopes and realized how vulnerable they were to ambush and attack from the heights all round them. Hannibal therefore decided to send his guides forward to reconnoitre before advancing with his main force any further. The news which the guides brought back was fairly encouraging, for it appeared that there was a pass and although it was defended in the day-time it was deserted at night, so that one bold move under cover of darkness should be enough to secure control of it. Hannibal pitched camp and waited for night to fall. Then, leaving the rest of his army with all their camp fires burning, he crept forward with a small group of volunteers and seized the top of the pass. But although the surprise was complete, the worst was not yet over. When daylight came and the rest of the army began to move forward to join them, they were fired at by Alpine tribesmen hidden on the hill-sides to right and left. The deafening noise as the shouts echoed from rock to rock caused the horses to panic and as they reared and plunged on the narrow path they threw the whole column into disorder. Men and animals were flung over the precipices which bordered the path and fell thousands of feet, like stones, to their death. The situation was saved by Hannibal who sent back a detachment of men from the head of the pass and dislodged the tribesmen from their vantage points.

For several days after this the army made good progress across a high plateau but Hannibal found on more than one occasion that he could not trust the local guides who often led him into traps

An Alpine pass

from which he only extricated himself with difficulty. It was here that the elephants which he had brought with him proved a useful deterrent. Although they were slow and clumsy along the steep tracks, they terrified the natives who had never seen anything like them before. At last, nine days after beginning the climb, the Carthaginian army reached the final summit. But bad as the climb had been, the descent proved much more difficult. Winter was beginning to set in and it began to snow in a steady blizzard which disheartened the soldiers as they struggled over the slippery ground. Even a brief glimpse which they had of the plains of Italy far below and the reassurance of Hannibal that there were no more hills to climb failed to cheer them up. They slid and stumbled down the slope, clutching at odd bushes and stumps to keep themselves from falling. In this way they got down a few thousand feet until they found that a landslide had carried away the track and they were faced with a yawning drop of nearly a hundred feet. The cavalry, who were leading the way, drew rein on the brink. It seemed impossible to advance and when Hannibal went forward to see for himself what was holding the army up, he decided that it was hopeless and that their only chance was to make a traverse across the bare hill-side. But this too proved useless. At first there were good footholds in the shallow layer of soft fresh snow which covered the old snow below but as soon as this had been trampled there was only bare ice and melting snow underneath. Some men tried to crawl across the slope on their hands and knees but if once they slipped there was nothing to stop them. A few managed to cut steps across to a gentler slope where the path began again. But most of them were too frightened even to try, especially when they saw the legs of the mules piercing the crust of hard ice and getting stuck fast so that they were quite unable to move.

 In face of this set-back Hannibal decided that they would have to rebuild the path where the landslide had destroyed it even though it was a tremendous job to hack a way down the cliff. He made a bivouac in the snow and organized the men into gangs to clear the ice and to cart away the debris. At one point the route was blocked by a mass of rock which he split in a most ingenious way. They cut down trees, piled them round the rock and lit a fire which a strong wind helped to blaze. This heated the rock. When it was nearly red-hot, they poured the men's rations of sour wine onto it and the rock split sufficiently for them to be able to cut a way through with picks and shovels. It took them four days to do it and during that time men and animals almost died of starvation because there is very little vegetation at that height and such as there was was covered by snow.

At last they got down, hungry and exhausted, into the warm, sunny valleys of Italy where pleasant streams flowed among rich woods and fields. It seemed like paradise to the Carthaginians after what they had put up with and for three whole days they rested thankfully. They had reached Italy. Rome was within their grasp.

In a series of well-planned engagements, at the River Ticinum and the River Trebia, Hannibal broke the main resistance of the Roman army in northern Italy and crossed the Apennines. There was now little to stop him from reaching Rome but his forces had been depleted during the hard winter and he had lost all the elephants that he had so laboriously brought over from Africa except for one. In order to safeguard his supply-line he had, therefore, to eliminate the one remaining Roman army in the field, that of the consul, C. Flaminius, which was based on Arrezzo. When he had done that, the way would be clear and unopposed.

Lake Trasimene

Fortunately for him the Romans played into his hands. It would have been their wisest policy to keep out of his range and to harass his communications with lightning strikes and not to run the risk of a full-scale action. But Flaminius was an ambitious and arrogant man whose head had been turned by some lucky successes in earlier wars. He was confident that he would do as well again this time. Hannibal knew what his opponent was like and aimed to provoke him into some foolish step by burning all the crops and the farms in the country-side round Arrezzo. This is one of the most fertile regions of Italy and it was more than Flaminius could stand to watch the smoke curling up from the fields while he did nothing to stop it. He regarded it as a slight on his honour to let the Carthaginians get away with such behaviour. So despite the unanimous advice of his staff who begged him not to do anything rash or at least to wait for reinforcements, Flaminius decided on instant action to put Hannibal in his place. Dismissing his council-of-war with a word, he issued orders that the army was to move at once and he himself jumped onto his horse to lead the way. But his horse slipped as he sprang into the saddle, and he fell heavily over its head onto the ground. This was hardly a good beginning and it was not made any better when the news came that the divisional standards were stuck so fast in the ground that they couldn't be moved. It looked as if the gods were doing everything in their power to prevent the army from leaving. But Flaminius angrily disregarded all this and curtly told the men to get some spades and dig the standards out. So at last they got under way.

Hannibal had carefully spread the trail of devastation from Arrezzo itself to the mountains round Lake Trasimene so as to bring Flaminius hot on his heels into an area where he could be trapped and ambushed. His plan succeeded. Ignoring the obvious signs that it was a trick, Flaminius marched straight for Lake Trasimene. The landscape here was rather like the Caudine Forks where a Roman army had been trapped a hundred years earlier. The road ran along the shore of the lake and for most of the way there was very little room between the water and the hills which rose up from

Lake Trasimene

the lake-side. But at one point the ground widened out into quite a large space before narrowing again where the hills came down right to the water's edge. It was a perfect place for an ambush. Hannibal camped with his African and Spanish troops in the wide field so that they should be plainly visible. The more agile irregulars he stationed behind the hills in a circle, while he concealed his cavalry at the narrow entrance to the field to cut the Roman retreat when they had passed.

Flaminius reached the lake at dawn next day. In his hurry he had not properly reconnoitred the route; there was a fine mist rising from the lake which cut visibility and the light was still too poor for him to see anything suspicious except the main Carthaginian force camped on the open ground. So he pressed eagerly forward through the narrow defile. This was just what Hannibal wanted.

As soon as he saw the Romans debouching into the field, he signalled to his cavalry to block the exit and for a general action to begin. Pandemonium broke out. The Romans were caught completely off-guard so that they had barely time to face about or to draw their swords, and despite the efforts of Flaminius, who rose magnificently to the occasion, they were unable to form a proper line of battle. The army split up into a series of small units fighting desperately for their lives against overwhelming odds. They were hemmed in by the mountains and the lake; they were blinded by the swirling mist; and they were hopelessly disorganized. But they refused to give in. For three hours they fought, no one more fiercely than Flaminius himself until a Gaul called Ducarius, who was serving in Hannibal's army, recognized his uniform and determined to get his revenge for all the injuries which the Gauls had received at Roman hands. He dug his spurs into his horse's flanks and charging full-tilt at Flaminius, struck down first of all his orderly and then the general himself. This broke the resistance of the Romans. They took to their heels and in their panic even tried to escape over the mountains or the lake. As a result thousands were drowned or sucked down by the mud, while those who went the other way slipped and fell to their death from the precipices. In all the Romans lost about 15,000 men and only a very few escaped to tell the tale. Even Hannibal was amazed when the sun dispersed the mist and he could see the full extent of his victory.

This might well have been the end of Rome but the command of what was left of the Roman army now devolved on a cautious general, called Q. Fabius Maximus who was the descendant of the sole survivor of the family of the Fabii which had perished at the Cremera 350 years before (see p. 43). Unlike Flaminius, Fabius refused to be provoked by Hannibal's atrocities. Patiently he shadowed the Carthaginian army all over Italy, never being drawn into battle but attacking stragglers and worrying the baggage-train whenever the chance presented itself. For time was on the side of the Romans. Hannibal's lines of communication were very long and he was getting short of men and ammunition. Besides his policy of 'scorched earth'—burning all the Italian farms —did himself as much harm as the Romans because it meant that his army could not live off the land but had to depend on supplies of food from overseas. Hannibal needed a quick result but it was just this that Fabius's tactics made impossible. So despite another great victory at Cannae (217 B.C.) and a sudden march on Rome which was nearly successful, the tide began to turn against Hannibal.

Fabius' tactics had earned him the nickname of 'Safety First' but gradually they began to pay dividends. Hannibal's progress was slowed, the Roman war-effort had a chance to recover and the Roman armies were re-equipped and reorganized. But, as often happens, the people became impatient with the speed at which things seemed to be going and felt that Fabius was unnecessarily cautious and defensive. Now was the time, they said, for vigorous action which would finish Hannibal off. There were a number of politicians at Rome, including a man called Varro, who had been brought up as a butcher's apprentice, who pressed for a change in the leadership of the war. After a series of popular demonstrations and public meetings they managed to get an act passed which effectively divided the command between Fabius and a junior colleague of his, Minucius, who had won a name for himself by some bold, but lucky, offensives. Fabius took this slight to himself calmly, recognising as always that the interests of the state were more important than his personal position. But Minucius was carried away by his promotion and at once began to draw up grandiose plans for beating Hannibal in the field. The first question, however, which they had to decide was how to exercise their joint command. When Minucius suggested that each should be supreme commander on alternate days or weeks, Fabius stoutly refused, saying that continuity was essential in the direction of a war and that he, for one, was not going to surrender any part of his joint responsibility. So they compromised in the end by dividing the army in half, each general being in command of two legions.

Hannibal could hardly believe his ears when it was reported that the Roman army had split up and was adopting different tactics. It was a golden opportunity, not to be missed, to isolate the two halves and defeat them separately. Moreover he was well aware that Minucius was rash and impetuous, the sort of general who could easily be led into a trap, while Fabius was now too weak to interfere with his movements. So he laid his plans for destroying Minucius.

Between the Carthaginians and Minucius' camp there was a small hill. It was at present unoccupied but both sides appreciated that they would gain a commanding position by occupying it. Hannibal toyed with the idea of seizing it but decided to use it instead as a bait to lure Minucius into an ambush. Although the valley leading up to the hill was bare and treeless, it was dotted with numerous rocky gullies and caves, some of them big enough to hold 200 men. Hannibal managed by night to conceal nearly 5,000 men in them without exciting Minucius' suspicion. Then he sent a small party at dawn to plant the Carthaginian flag on top of the hill. As he had hoped, this cheeky act infuriated Minucius, who instantly sent a substantial part of his army to dislodge the Carthaginians and to capture the hill. The Carthaginians, however, in retaliation sent up reinforcements to support their advance party which obliged Minucius to commit the rest of his army to the action. No sooner had the whole of Minucius' army passed through the valley to begin the assault on the hill than Carthaginians, who were in hiding, rose up behind them and fell on them with a roar. Panic at once broke out and it was only a matter of time before Minucius and all his men would have been massacred had the sound of the battle not reached Fabius' ears in his own camp several miles away. Sensing immediately that his colleague had been guilty of some act of bravado, he moved his men with lightning speed towards the scene, where his unexpected appearance rallied Minucius' soldiers and caused Hannibal to break off the action. Many Romans had been killed but the day was saved.

The event brought Minucius to his senses. He reunited his troops with Fabius' and resigned his share of the command. He saw now that while Fabius had acted all along like a wise and far-seeing father, he had behaved like a silly, spoiled child. He had learned his lesson.

Meanwhile a new generation of generals grew up at Rome, among whom Scipio and Marcellus made the greatest mark.

Scipio and Allucius

Scipio was the most enterprising of these generals. He realized that the key to final victory over the Carthaginians lay not so much in defeating Hannibal's army in Italy as in breaking the Carthaginian empire in Spain, Sicily and Africa. So he persuaded the Romans to send one of their newly formed armies to Spain under his command. It seemed at first a foolish thing to do to leave Hannibal, still undefeated, roaming at will throughout Italy but events proved Scipio right. By a series of hard-fought actions he gained control of much of Spain and by 210 B.C. had succeeded in cutting Hannibal's supply routes and threatened Carthage itself. It began to look as if Hannibal would have to withdraw from Italy in order to save Carthage.

Despite Scipio's brilliance as a soldier he is chiefly remembered today for his kindness and statesmanship. Livy tells the story of his behaviour after a great victory in Spain where thousands of prisoners were captured, among them a large number of women hostages.

It was Scipio's policy, wherever possible, to win people over by friendliness rather than force them to obey against their will. He saw an opportunity here of making himself popular with the local Spanish tribes by returning the hostages to their own homes instead of selling them into slavery as many other generals would have done. So he drew up a list of them all by nationality and sent word to their government at home to arrange transport to take them back. He promised that he would look after them in the meanwhile until people came to collect them. This was in itself a very decent thing to do but Scipio went even further. One of the hostages, the wife of a Spanish prince and a woman of some age, came to him with tears in her eyes and said that she didn't care what happened to her personally—she was too old—but she was frightened what might happen to some of the others, who were young and beautiful, if they were left in charge of rough and coarse soldiers. Scipio saw the point at once and entrusted them to the care of a responsible and senior officer who was to treat them like his own family.

One of the girls was remarkably pretty and drew everyone's eyes on her wherever she walked. Scipio was intrigued to know who she was and where she came from. So he called her up and began to ask her questions. He found out that she was engaged to a young Spanish prince called Allucius whom she very much wanted to marry. Scipio, who was only about thirty-six years old himself, felt so sorry for her that he at once arranged for her parents and her fiancé to be fetched. When Allucius arrived, Scipio took him on one side and, having satisfied himself that he was genuinely in love with the girl, said to him: 'We are both young, so there is no need for us to be embarrassed by this conversation. When I found out that she loved you and that you returned her love, I wanted to do everything in my power to bring you both together again. After all, I know the unhappiness of separated loves all too well. Here am I, hundreds of miles from home and family. So take her and good luck to you! I can assure you that she has come to no harm while she has been with us. I only ask for one thing in return, that from now you should be friends with Rome. The Romans are not brutes, as you often imagine. Most of them are just like me and only want the world to be happy and peaceful.' Allucius broke down with surprise and joy. He grasped Scipio's hand and said he didn't see how he could ever be good enough to repay Scipio's kindness but with the gods' help he would try his utmost. The two men then returned to her parents and broke the news to them. They had brought a large sum of money with them in case they had to ransom her, which they now pressed on Scipio as a token of their gratitude. They were so insistent that Scipio felt he had to accept it but he took it and handed it to Allucius, explaining that he should regard it as a wedding-present from him.

This gesture—which was typical of Scipio—deeply impressed the Spanish and did much to make them support Rome instead of Carthage.

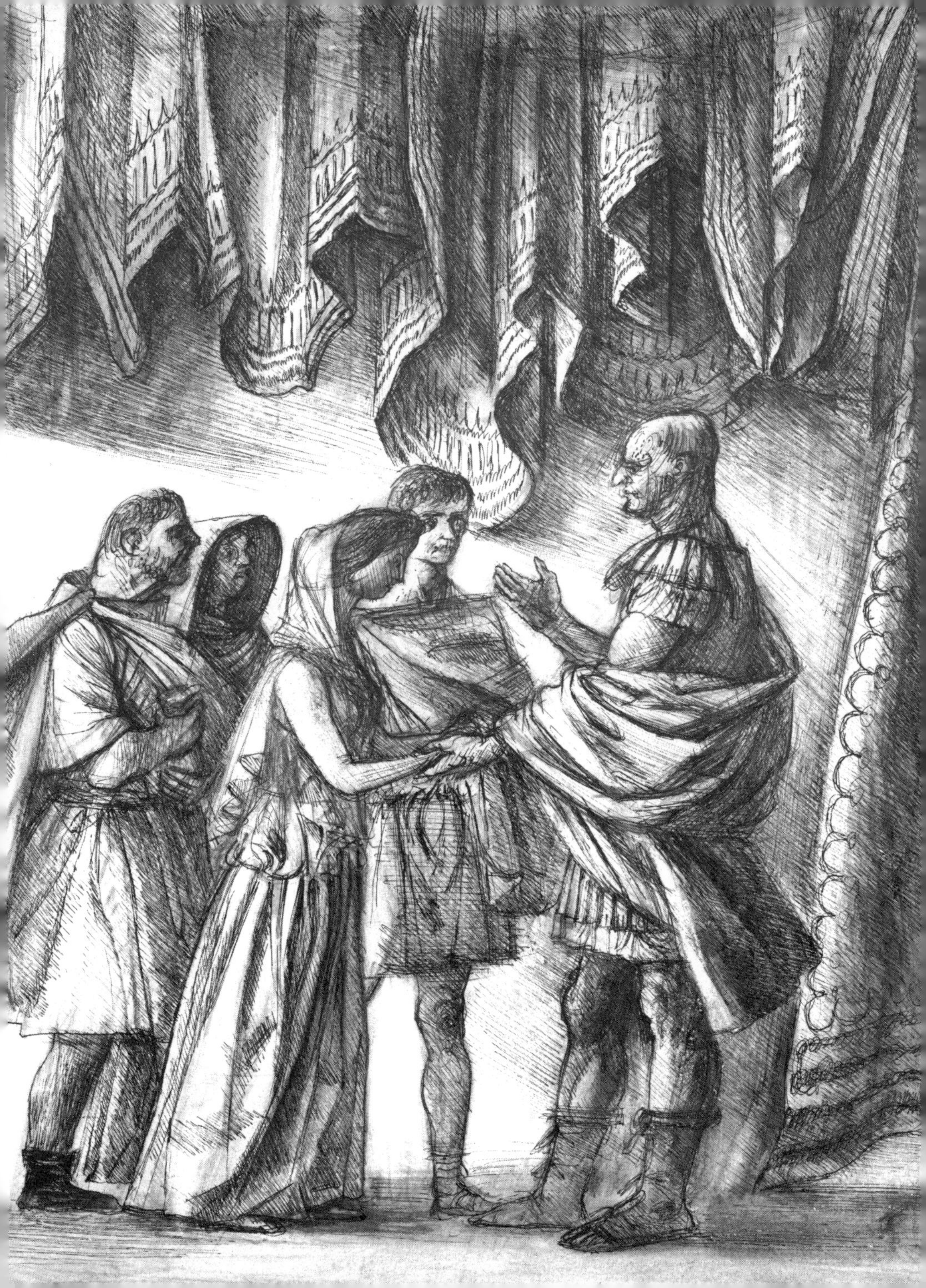

The Story of Sophonisba

The tide of war was turning in favour of the Romans. The Carthaginian leader Syphax had been defeated in Numidia by the Roman commander Laelius and his Numidian ally Masinissa. Masinissa was overjoyed as his father had once ruled in Numidia. He asked Laelius to allow him to ride on ahead to the capital, Cirta, taking with him the defeated Syphax in chains.

When he reached the city the sight of their defeated king struck terror into the hearts of the citizens and Masinissa easily assumed control. As he entered the palace he was met by Sophonisba, the wife of Syphax and daughter of Hasdrubal the Carthaginian. Sophonisba was a great beauty and well aware of her powers to charm men. She fell on her knees before Masinissa. She begged him to save her from being carried off as a slave by the Romans.

Masinissa fell, at once, a victim to her charms. He gave her his hand and promised she would never be given to a Roman. Instead he decided to marry her himself that very day. He ordered that preparations should be made at once. By the time Laelius had reached the city, they were married.

Laelius was furious but could do nothing but await the arrival of Scipio from Spain. Meanwhile Syphax was brought to the Roman camp, still in chains and followed by a company of noble Numidians. It was a victory for the Romans over both the Carthaginians and the Numidians.

When Scipio saw the plight of the defeated Syphax he felt very sorry for him, for he had known and respected him in the past. Why, he asked, had he been so foolish as to wage war against the Romans? Syphax blamed his marriage with the Carthaginian woman, Sophonisba. She had led him astray by her beauty and her wiles just as she was now corrupting the young Numidian prince, Masinissa. His words were bitter for he still loved his beautiful wife who had betrayed him.

Scipio was deeply affected by what Syphax told him. He summoned Masinissa to his tent and praised him for his valour. But he spoke severely of his conduct in taking Sophonisba as his share of the spoil when she should have been sent as a slave to Rome with the other captives.

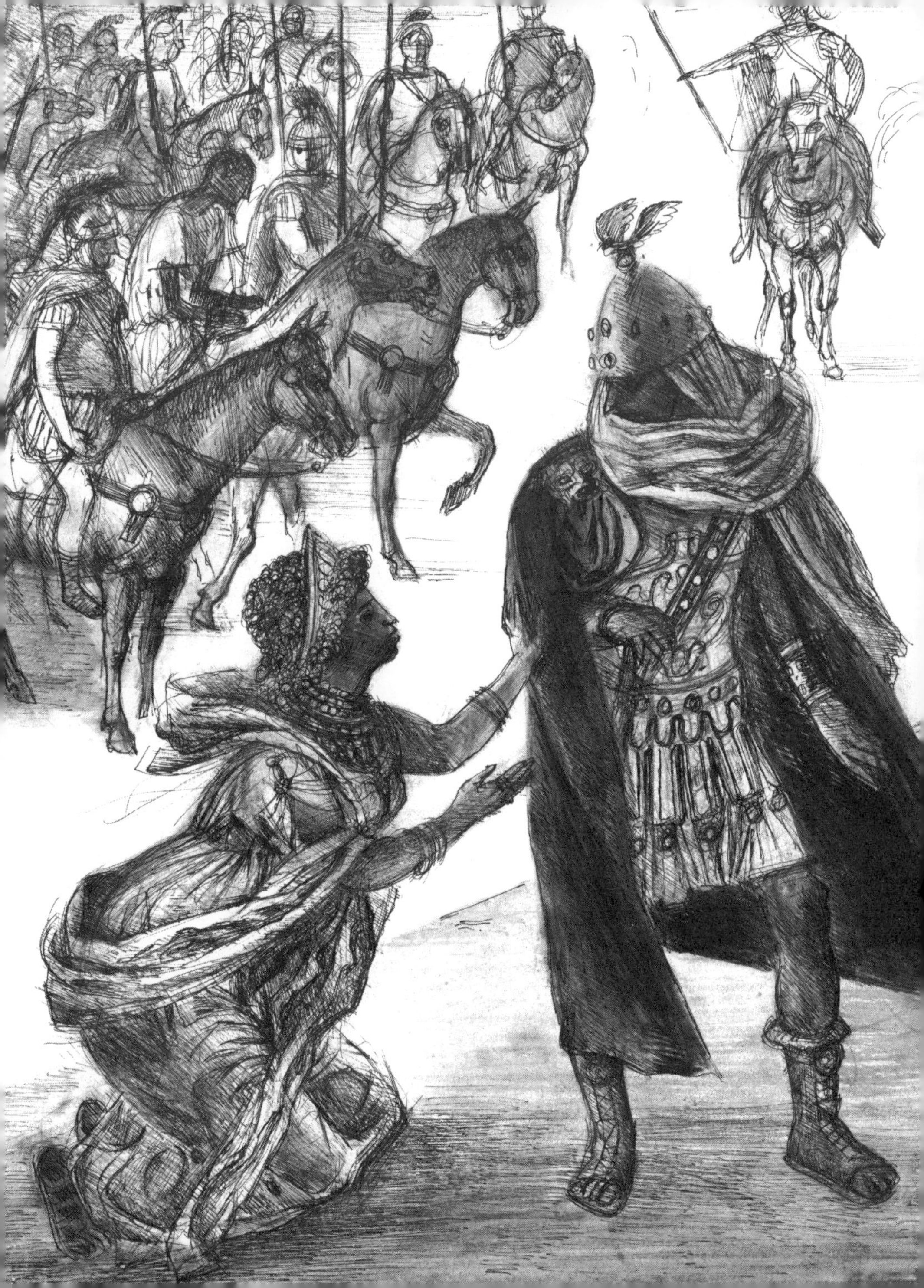

Masinissa took Scipio's warning to heart. He saw that his reputation was seriously in danger and he must get rid of Sophonisba. At the same time he remembered his promise to her that she would never fall into Roman hands. There was only one thing to be done. He summoned a trusty slave and got him to prepare a cup of poisoned wine and take it to Sophonisba. She would know what she must do if she was to escape a life of slavery.

Sophonisba received the cup of wine and realized what it meant for her. With great dignity she took it and drank it to the dregs.

When Scipio heard of this he was afraid that Masinissa would kill himself in grief for the loss of his bride. He comforted him with kindly words and gave him rich presents—embroidered clothes and a golden crown. Masinissa saw that he might still become king of Numidia. Although Sophonisba had died, the future was still bright for him.

The Siege of Syracuse

In the war between Rome and Carthage, the island of Sicily lying midway between the great powers, played an unwilling part. Syracuse, a wealthy merchant city and the largest in the island, was open to bribes from both sides. At first she was an ally of Rome but she fell a prey to fair promises from Carthage and allowed the Carthaginian fleet to use her splendid harbour. The Romans, realising the danger, sent their best general, Marcus Marcellus, to Sicily to restore their power in the island.

The city of Syracuse was torn into two factions. Many of the citizens would have liked to return to the Roman alliance. Others were swayed by the skilful speeches of Hippocrates and Epicydes, the agents of Hannibal. These men stirred up the common people in the name of liberty. They told terrible stories of the punishment they might expect if the Romans returned to the city. The result was that the chief magistrates, who favoured the Roman cause, were put to death and war was declared on Rome. The Carthaginians, Hippocrates and Epicydes, declared themselves governors of the city.

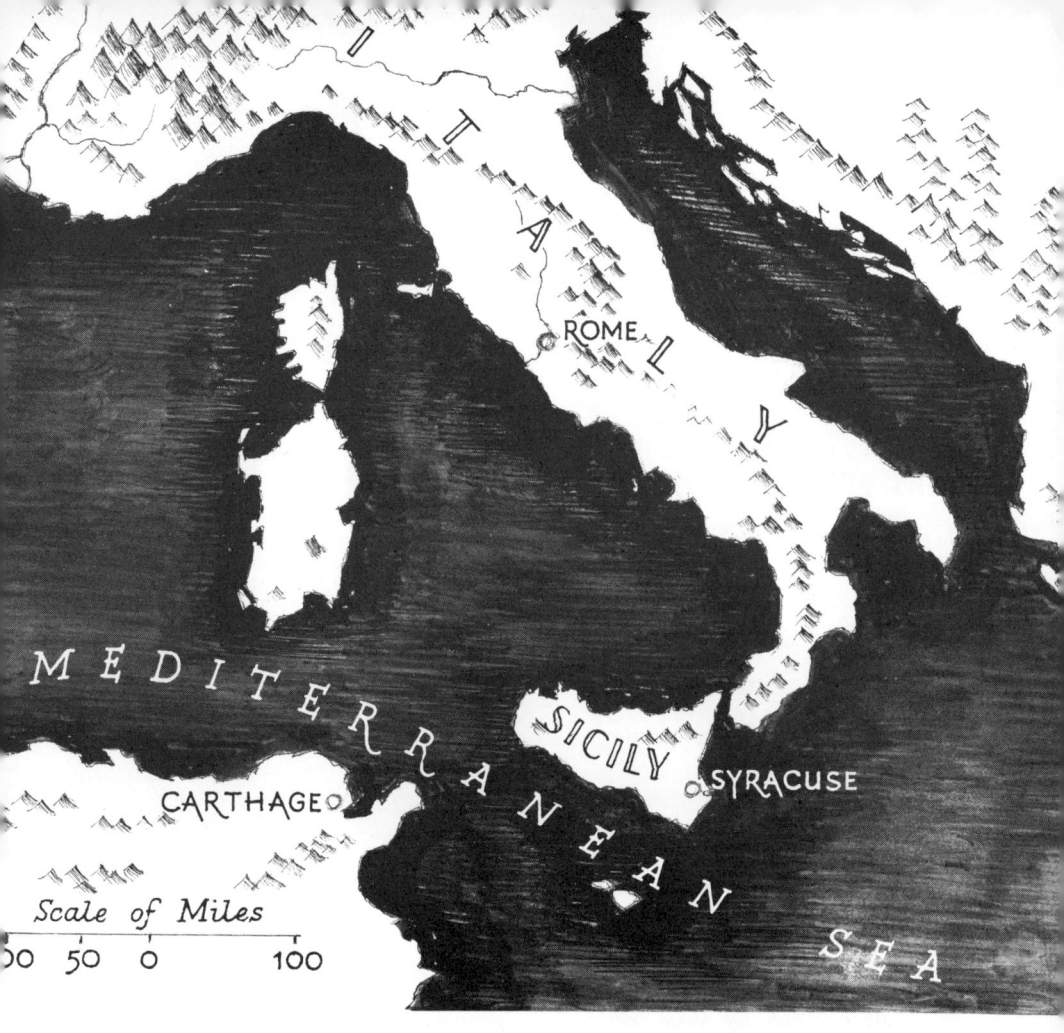

The Mediterranean

No course was left to Marcellus but to lay siege to Syracuse. The city might have fallen at once but for the fact that its defence was directed by Archimedes, the celebrated mathematician and engineer. By the ingenious artillery he had invented he successfully held the Romans at bay. He used both heavy and light cannon; the heavy hurled stones of enormous size, the light could be hauled into all sorts of unlikely places and fired at frequent intervals. He

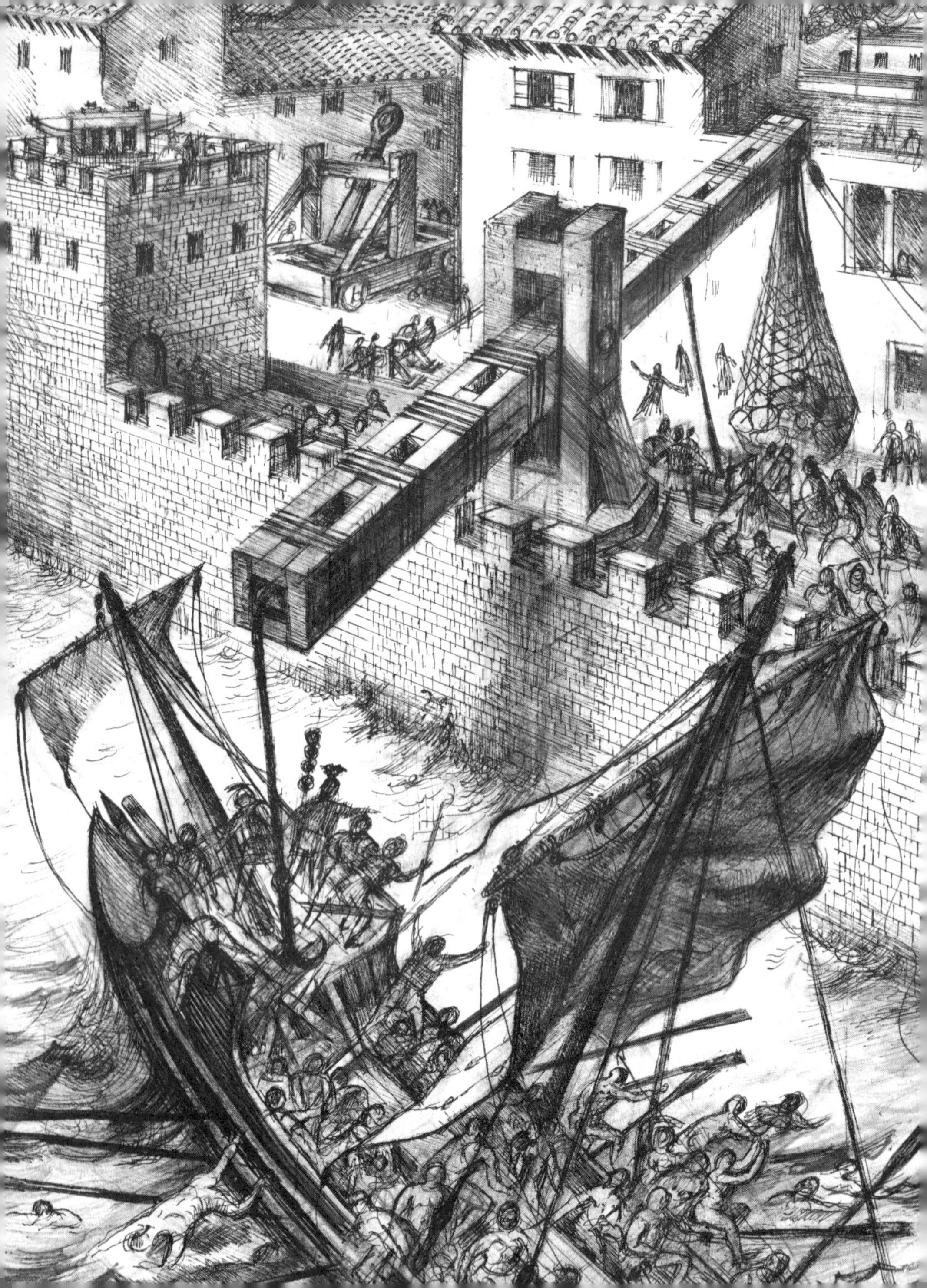

also invented a very useful grappling iron which seized the enemy ships when they came close to the walls, upended them, and smashed them to pieces. The siege, as a result, lasted for eight months and had to be converted into a blockade by sea and land by the Romans.

Meanwhile the Carthaginians hearing how well the garrison at Syracuse was doing, sent a strong army to Sicily under General Hamilco. Hippocrates marched out of the city to join him. The position of Marcellus between the defenders of Syracuse and two hostile armies was critical. He held his ground, with difficulty, and continued his blockade of Syracuse. He also carried out raids on neighbouring towns and brought them again under Roman rule. At last, two years later, in 212 B.C., Marcellus saw his chance to take the city. He heard from a deserter that the festival of Diana was in full swing in Syracuse and the defenders were enjoying the celebrations, drinking more wine than they had done since the siege started.

Marcellus chose a picked band of men, who at a sign from him, when night had fallen, succeeded in scaling the outer walls. In single file they slipped silently past the sleeping sentries. Just before dawn Marcellus reached the heights of Epipolae, in the suburbs of the city and looked down on the city below him, one of the most beautiful in the world. As he stood there he wept, remembering the city's ancient glory when Athens and Carthage had fallen to her power.

In vain Marcellus tried to induce the garrison to surrender and prevent further bloodshed. They would not yield to him. An attempt by Hippocrates and Hamilco, aided by the Carthaginian fleet, to save the city failed. The relieving armies were obliged to camp in the low marshy grounds on the banks of the river Anapus. In hot summer weather, disease broke out. Marcellus and his Romans quartered in the higher ground of the suburbs suffered little, but fevers ravaged the armies of the Carthaginians and their Sicilian allies. Hippocrates and Hamilco both died of plague and the remnant of their armies scattered over Sicily. The city surrendered to the Romans. Unfortunately Marcellus spoiled his reputation by allowing the troops to loot the shops and houses and in the resulting wave of violence Archimedes and many other citizens were killed. It is said that Archimedes was busy working out sums with figures he had traced in the dust and did not notice the hideous uproar in the city. He was killed by a soldier who did not know who he was. Marcellus was distressed by this and gave him an honourable burial. With his death and the capture of the city, the great days of Syracuse were gone for ever.

A Mutiny

It would be quite wrong to imagine that the Romans were perfect or to think that their leaders were always in full control of things. Like everyone else they had their ups and downs. In a war as lengthy as the second Carthaginian war it was inevitable that there should be some serious setbacks. Here Livy tells how Scipio had to face a mutiny by his own soldiers which threatened to undo all the progress which he had made.

In 206 B.C. Scipio, who had almost brought the war in Spain to a successful end, fell seriously ill and, as so often happens, rumour made people believe that he was much worse than he really was. His illness had disastrous consequences for the country. A number of Spanish princes, who had reluctantly made peace with the Romans, thought that Scipio was dying and that this was their chance to break away from Rome and set up independent kingdoms. It had still worse effect on the Roman army itself, which was already somewhat demoralized as a result of a long period of inactivity; for war keeps men on the stretch and gives them a variety of excitement and interests, whereas an army in peacetime is easily bored by dull routine, especially when it is a conscript army which feels that it should be demobilized as soon as the war has been won.

Discipline in one of the large Roman garrisons, some 8,000 strong at Sucro in southern Spain, began to break down. The soldiers started answering the officers back; they went absent without leave, looting in the surrounding country-side; they demanded higher pay. Eventually they evicted their own officers from the camp and replaced them with a couple of brash privates, called Albius and Atrius ('Whitey' and 'Blackie'), who not only took charge but even had the face to appear in officers' uniform. Like most revolutionaries they hoped to turn the general chaos to their own profit. It was their intention to line their own pockets as fast as they could and then quietly to disappear.

But things did not develop according to plan. The expected news of Scipio's death never came; the widespread breakdown of law and order on which they were counting did not happen. Instead the soldiers began to get cold feet at the thought of what they had done and slunk back to their old officers leaving 'Whitey' and 'Blackie' in solitary splendour. The officers, sensing that this was the psychological moment, made thorough and understanding inquiries into the soldiers' grievances which were—as could have been guessed—that their pay was late and that they had not received proper recognition for their contribution to the Roman victory. The officers promised to report the grievances at once to the commander-in-chief, Scipio, assuring the men confidently that they would be dealt with without delay.

It was the first time that Scipio had had to cope with such a problem, but, feeling that the chief priority was to prevent the trouble from spreading, he made special efforts to collect enough money to meet the pay claims in the near future and then worked out a plan for dealing with the troublemakers. He discovered that the real ring-leaders in the army totalled a mere thirty-five soldiers, while

Spain

the rest had followed their lead blindly. So he decided to take action only against the thirty-five but to give the others a short, sharp lesson. He let it be known that he was going to transfer the mutinous army to New Carthage, the capital of southern Spain, to relieve the army at present quartered there for service against the rebel Spanish princes. In fact this was all a trick; for the princes had already made their own terms with Scipio as soon as they heard of his recovery, and his real purpose was to get the mutineers firmly into his power. But the mutinous army welcomed the move, because they thought that it meant that they were going to be paid and that they would be able to bring extra pressure to bear on Scipio, if they got him alone. So they marched with a swagger to New Carthage to find the other army packing up and preparing to leave. The occasion seemed to call for a party to celebrate the hand-over and, on Scipio's orders, the new arrivals were all invited by the departing army to join them in a few drinks. The thirty-five troublemakers were split up and taken to the quarters of seven of Scipio's most trusted officers. They thought that they were going for a quiet evening's entertainment but, when they got there, they were instantly overpowered and clapped into irons. The rest of the soldiers were lulled by drink into a complacent and unsuspecting frame of mind, so that next morning they watched with a light heart as their hosts formed up into column of march and made as if to leave the town on their way to the battlefront. But Scipio had other ideas. Just as they were passing through the gates, he halted them and silently posted guards on all the main gateways of the town to prevent anyone from trying to escape.

Then he summoned the mutineers to parade unarmed before him. While they were gathering in a noisy, disorganized crowd, without any semblance of discipline or formation, Scipio brought the main body of his loyal soldiers back from the gates and stationed them in a ring round them. This unexpected sight was too much for them. Their defiance vanished on the spot. Instead they were gripped by shame and fear, especially when they saw Scipio mount the platform as fit as ever but with a look of fury in his eyes which they could not remember having seen even in the heat of battle.

For several minutes he took them to task for their utter folly and stupidity. What could they possibly have hoped to gain by their behaviour? Did they really want to live the rest of their lives in a squalid little place like Sucro? Or did they believe that a few thousand men with such paltry leaders as 'Blackie' and 'Whitey' could detach the whole of Spain from the Roman empire and turn it into an independent state. 'Words fail me' he said, 'to describe my feelings that soldiers, whom I trusted and whom I thought that I knew, should be guilty of such treason against their country. Yet it is not all your fault. A crowd is like the sea which has no motion of its own but is stirred by winds whether light or strong. You too have your calms and your storms but the handful of men who were the cause of this fit of madness shall not escape so lightly. If you now regret what you have done, that is in itself adequate punishment; but the ring-leaders shall pay for it with their lives.'

His words had a sobering effect which was strengthened by the frightening sight which followed. To the accompaniment of a great din from the loyal soldiers as they beat their swords against their shields, the thirty-five ring-leaders were dragged into the middle. There, in the sight of everyone, they were stripped and bound to stakes and then whipped and beheaded.

Scipio had no more trouble from the army after that.

The Battle of the Metaurus

The Carthaginians were increasingly alarmed at the way things were going. Hannibal was cut off in Italy, Sicily had virtually been lost and much of Spain was now in Roman hands. So they decided to make one more big effort to send an army to reinforce Hannibal and to stake everything on a massive attack on Rome. This army set out from Carthage through Spain under the command of Hannibal's brother, Hasdrubal. After great difficulty it crossed the Alps into Italy but before it could join up with Hannibal it was met and defeated by the two Roman generals, Claudius and Livius, at the river Metaurus in the year 207 B.C.

The battle was the result of some very quick thinking by the Romans. Claudius with one army was in the south of Italy, carefully shadowing Hannibal, while Livius was in the north waiting for the arrival of Hasdrubal. But a stroke of luck gave Claudius a rare chance to break the deadlock. He had intercepted two messengers who were bringing a letter from Hasdrubal to Hannibal with the good news of his approach. Claudius realized that if he acted quickly he could link up with Livius and beat Hasdrubal two to one, before Hannibal even knew that his brother had arrived safely in Italy. It was a very bold step to take because it meant leaving only a token force to watch Hannibal while he took the rest of the army at high speed northwards. Indeed when the government at Rome heard of Claudius's plan, they were tempted to veto it as being too risky. But by then it was already too late. Selecting the toughest of his troops Claudius had set out under cover of darkness from his base near Canusium and Hannibal never discovered until long afterwards what was happening.

Claudius's march was a remarkable demonstration of how much the Romans were liked and the Carthaginians hated. At every stage, people streamed from the fields and villages to line the road and to cheer the soldiers on their way. They offered them horses; they pressed food and wine on them; they wished them every success. The soldiers acknowledged their goodwill but it was a race against time and they could only stop for occasional rests. So the long column of men tramped steadily northwards.

Claudius had warned Livius that he was coming and the news posed a difficult problem. Livius wondered whether he should build an extra camp in readiness for them (which would warn Hasdrubal that the Romans had a large army in the field and perhaps scare him away) or whether he should try and conceal the fact that his army was going to be almost doubled in size. In the end they decided to keep Claudius's arrival dark, especially since Hasdrubal's army was now camped near Sena only about half-a-mile away. So it was arranged that when Claudius had caught up, he should keep his troops out of sight behind a low range of hills until nightfall; then the soldiers would be smuggled silently into Livius' camp and the two armies would share one set of tents for the night. The trick worked and, as a result, the junction of the two armies was not detected by Hasdrubal. Despite the discomfort of having to double up, all the Romans managed to find quarters within the one camp. A feeling of suppressed excitement ran throughout the whole army and morale was so high that the generals agreed not to wait until Claudius' troops had recovered from the journey but to strike at once while the surprise was complete.

So next day the signal was given to be ready for battle and Hasdrubal, on his side, was keen not to waste time but to have it out at once. But just as he was making his final preparations, he began to have suspicions. The Roman army looked larger than before; their horses were leaner; and he thought he spotted some shields which he had not seen previously and which he did not recognize. So at the last moment he drew back. Instead he sent some observers forward, with orders to spy out whether the camp had been enlarged during the night, to make a note of the bugle-calls, and to spot any particularly sun-burned soldiers who might have just made a long march, and, if possible, to capture a few prisoners for interrogation. His suspicions were confirmed when the scouts reported that, although the camp had not been enlarged, they had distinctly heard double bugle-calls which could only mean that both the consuls were present. A dozen fears ran through Hasdrubal's mind, but of one thing he was clear. Something awful must have happened to Hannibal, for otherwise Claudius would never have come from the south.

In this uncertainty the only thing to do was to make a rapid get-away. When night fell, he put out the fires and told his troops to pick up their equipment silently and to strike camp. But a night-march is always tricky and he had not gone far before the trouble began. The guides deserted; the soldiers started to straggle and began to lose touch with each other; some were so tired after the day's exertions that they just lay down quietly and went to sleep on the ground. Above all the route was very heavy going. He had meant to cross the river Metaurus but, having lost his guides, he had missed the ford and had to continue along the bank. This was very twisty and steep so that his progress was pitifully slow.

Next day the Romans soon caught up with them and Hasdrubal had to turn and fight. His men put up a good show despite their exhaustion and the unaccustomed heat, but it was the elephants that really kept the Romans at bay until they got out of control and started to run amok all over the place. Then the mahouts had no choice but to kill them which they did by driving a chisel with a heavy mallet into the joint between the head and the neck. The loss of so many elephants swung the battle round and the Carthaginians began to give way. In a last attempt to save the day, Hasdrubal led a desperate charge and died valiantly at the head of his men. After that all organized resistance was broken. The battle degenerated into a massacre in which over 56,000 Carthaginians were killed and 5,400 taken prisoner. Livius even allowed a party of Gauls, who could easily have been ridden down, to escape in order, as he said, that there should be some survivors to tell Hannibal the size of the defeat. But in fact Hannibal heard the news in a more gruesome way. As soon as the battle was over, Claudius collected his men and began his return journey which he completed within a week— even quicker than on the way up. He took with him Hasdrubal's head, carefully wrapped up, and when he got back, he rolled it into Hannibal's camp to tell its own story.

After the destruction of Hasdrubal's army things went from bad to worse for Hannibal and the Carthaginians. They were cut off from home without any prospect of getting help or supplies. But for four more years he managed to maintain his position in southern Italy until in 203 B.C. he was recalled to defend Carthage itself against Scipio who had landed in Africa with a large Roman army. During these years he tried to persuade several of the great kings of the Middle East to take up arms against Rome. One of these was an ambitious but weak king, Philip the Fifth of Macedon, who had made an alliance with Hannibal in the hope of making himself master of the whole of Greece as a result. Philip fought against the Romans from 215 to 205 B.C. but despite a few local successes he was unable to make much headway, chiefly because his position was always threatened by bitter family quarrels. These can best be imagined from the story of the jealousy of Philip's two sons, Perseus and Demetrius, which, as Livy tells, came to a head a few years later.

Perseus and Demetrius

Perseus was the elder son, about thirty years old, a fine upstanding man who was proud of the independence of his country from Rome and who hoped, when his turn came to be king, to follow the line which his father had taken. Demetrius, who was some five years younger, had spent several years in Rome as a political hostage, during which he had acquired the manners and the culture of a Roman gentleman as well as coming to see that there was no future in a small country like Macedon deliberately opposing or provoking Rome. Demetrius was intelligent, well educated and charming so that it was not long before he had gained a wide following in Macedon who felt that their future would be more secure if he rather than his brother were to be the next king. Philip was now an old man and the question of the royal succession was causing a good deal of public anxiety. People were weighing up the undoubted right of

Perseus as the older son against the advantages which would follow if Demetrius, the recognized friend of Rome, were to succeed instead. Perseus sensed that public opinion was running against him so that he would have to do something drastic if his claim was not to be passed over. He began by approaching a few prominent men and trying to enlist their support. Whatever their real feelings may have been, most of them were only anxious to keep in with the present king and since they were well aware that he distrusted the Romans, they were prepared to back Perseus and his policies just as long as they saw that these were approved by the king. Perseus now saw that everything turned on poisoning his father's mind against Rome and against everything pro-Roman. He used to drag into casual conversation disparaging remarks about the Romans, running down their achievements and their civilization and decrying their leaders. This technique was greatly assisted by the fact that Demetrius always sprang to the defence of the Romans until he made himself thoroughly unpopular with his father and was excluded from all share in the government. The way was now clear for Perseus to work on his father's fears and suspicions—which he did to great effect. Whenever the king negotiated a foreign alliance or discussed ways and means of damaging the Romans, Perseus would always remind him that he should beware of dangers nearer at hand: there was an enemy spy within his own house.

Shortly afterwards there was a military review. Traditionally the parade and religious ceremonies at such reviews were followed by a mock battle-exercise. On this occasion the opposing sides were led by Perseus and Demetrius respectively, but such was the feeling between the two princes and their contingents that the exercise practically turned into a pitched fight and, despite the fact that only dummy weapons were used, quite a lot of blood was actually shed. The outcome, however, was decisively in favour of Demetrius. In the evening a number of informal parties were given to enable the soldiers to relax after all their exertions. Demetrius invited Perseus to have dinner with him but he refused the invitation, sending instead one of his agents in the hope of picking up some treasonable gossip at Demetrius' party. Unfortunately the agent was detected and roughly thrown out by some of Demetrius' rather

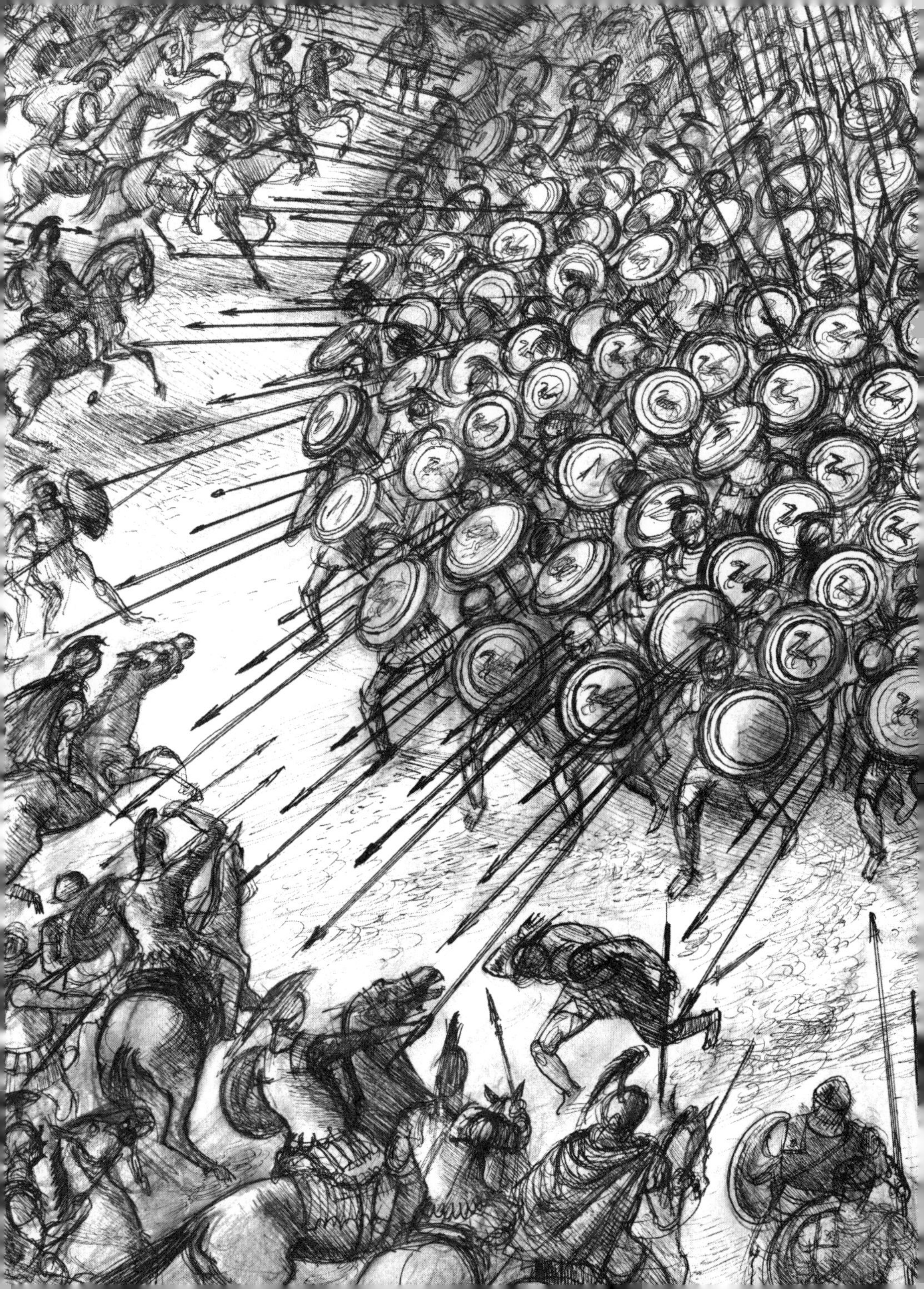

drunken guests. As the evening wore on and the wine flowed, Demetrius felt increasingly guilty that his side had won and in the end suggested that they should all go and join Perseus' party, to make it up with him and show that there were no ill feelings. His friends said that this was a splendid idea but a few of them, especially those who had manhandled the gate-crasher, thought privately that it would be as well to go armed—just to be on the safe side. This was noticed and quickly reported to Perseus, who, fearing the worst, locked his doors and gave orders that no one was to be admitted. After a certain amount of disorderly shouting and swearing Demetrius made his way home again.

Next day Perseus complained openly to his father that he had only narrowly escaped from an attempt on his life. He asked how long his father was going to tolerate such anarchy. Philip was naturally worried and agreed to set up a court of inquiry to investigate the charge. He invited two retired statesmen, Lysimachus and Onomastus, who were no longer personally involved in politics, to join him as assessors. Then he sent for Demetrius and Perseus. Perseus arrived at once with three lawyers and a carefully prepared speech; Demetrius with difficulty got out of bed, was quite unprepared and came just as he was, dishevelled and suffering badly from a hang-over. Philip began the proceedings with a short speech in which he stressed the sadness that the occasion made him feel. He had noticed the ill-feeling between his two sons but he had hoped that it would pass as they remembered their happy childhood together or reflected on the many examples which history afforded of spectacular successes brought about by teamwork between brothers. His hopes had been dashed: their savage rivalry was obviously too bitter to be ended peacefully; therefore, he had decided to hear both sides of the quarrel in open court and to give judgement.

His two sons then presented their cases. Perseus began by protesting that *he* did not need to make any defence of his conduct: he was the innocent victim, set upon in the middle of the night by a gang of thugs led by his so-called brother who, knowing that he could never be king of Macedon by right, had resorted to murder in order to eliminate his rival. There were plenty of witnesses who would confirm in detail what had happened. He doubted whether even Demetrius would have the nerve to deny it. But the plot was not as simple as that. Demetrius was in the pay of the Romans and their general, Quinctius Flamininus, who were using him as a pawn to get the whole of Macedon for themselves. 'Only your life, father, and mine', he ended, 'stand between the Romans and their goal'.

There was a prolonged silence when Perseus finished and all eyes turned to see how Demetrius would reply to this attack. For some time he was too overcome with emotion to speak, until a direct order brought him to his feet. Then in simple words which were all the more effective because they were so obviously unrehearsed, he demolished Perseus' insinuations by showing how ridiculous it would have been to choose a public holiday for an assassination or for the conspirators to get drunk before undertaking such a dangerous and delicate job. His willingness to leave home and go as a political hostage to Rome proved that there was no more loyal and patriotic subject of his father than he. He had no wish to make matters worse by bringing counter-charges against his brother. Instead he left it to the king to make up his own mind who was in the right and who was in the wrong.

It was a most impressive performance which left Philip in an uncomfortable position. The future of Macedon depended on this quarrel being resolved once and for all but Philip did not have the courage to face up to it. Mumbling a few words to the effect that this was a very important matter which must not be decided in a hurry but should be carefully considered from every angle, he weakly let the chance slip. So things in Macedon went on just as before.

The Death of Hannibal

After Philip was forced to make peace with the Romans in 205 B.C. it was only a matter of time before the Carthaginians were finally defeated. Scipio annihilated Hannibal's army at Zama, near the gates of Carthage, in 202 B.C. and the most serious war in Rome's history was over. Hannibal however managed to escape to the East where he was welcomed by King Antiochus of Syria whom he persuaded to renew the fight against Rome. But the Romans were now so strong and so confident that Antiochus' power was soon broken and in 190 B.C. Hannibal found himself a refugee once again. This time he was given asylum by the king of Bithynia, Prusias, but his stay there was short-lived. The Romans began to close in on him and in 182 B.C. he was eventually cornered when the Roman commander, Quinctius Flamininus, arrived at the court of Prusias and demanded Hannibal's surrender.

Hannibal was too experienced to have much faith in the word of a king. He knew that the Romans would never rest until he was dead and he knew that Prusias would not risk his throne by antagonizing the Romans. So although Prusias had solemnly promised that he would protect him, Hannibal never trusted him and had taken various precautions of his own. He had, for instance, built himself a special house with seven different exits, several of which were secret so that, if ever the need arose, he could escape unobserved. But all these ingenious devices were in vain. After a short discussion Prusias agreed to hand over Hannibal to Flamininus and sent a body of soldiers to Hannibal's house to arrest him. Suspecting that he might try to escape, they put guards and roadblocks on all the roads that led to the house and posted a ring of soldiers right round it. Then the officer in charge, with a few men, knocked on the front door. When Hannibal was told that an officer wanted to see him, he at once tried to slip out by one of the secret passages but he found that every route was guarded and blocked and that there was no chance of escape. So he returned to the house and asked one of the servants to bring him the poison which he always kept ready for such an emergency. If the Romans could not wait for an old man to die naturally, he would at least deprive them of the satisfaction of killing him: the rest of the world would not think it a very creditable achievement that they had only managed to get rid of him at last when he was alone, one against thousands, and betrayed by his host. With a gesture of defiance he drained his glass. So died the most dangerous enemy that Rome ever had to face.

Index

Aeneas, 2
Aeneid, 2
Aequi, 38
Alba Longa, 6–8, 16–20
Alban Lake, 53–4
Albius, 105
Allobroges tribe, 84
Allucius, 94–6
Alps, 82 ff.
Amulius, 6–8
Anapus, river, 103
Antium, 40
Apollo, 55–6
Appenines, 88
Apulia, 73, 74
Archimedes, 101, 103
Ardea, 30
Arrezzo, 89
Arruns, 25–6
Atrius, 105
Augustus, 1, 2
Aventine Hill, 8, 57

Brennus, 61

Cacus, 9–10
Caere, 21, 32, 34
Caesar, 1
Camillus, *see* Furius
Carthage, 82
Carthaginians, 82 ff.
Cincinnatus, 2, 4, 44–5, 49–50
Claudius, 109–113
Claudius, Appius, 46–7
Cloelia, 36–8
Clusium, 59
Collatinus, 30–2
Coriolanus, Gnaeus Marcius, *see* Marcius
Corioli, 38–9
Corvinus, 69
Cremera, river, 43
Curiatii, 16–18

Decius, 79–82
Delphi, 52, 53
Demetrius, 113–17
Druentia, river, 84
Ducarius, 91

Epicydes, 100
Esquiline hill, 11
Etruscans, 21 ff.
Evander, 10

Fabii, 42–3
Fabius C. Dorsus, 60
Fabius, Q., 79–81, 91–4
Falerii, 57
Faustulus, 5, 7
Flaminius, C., 89–91
Furius, L. Camillus, 66–7
Furius, M. Camillus, 2, 4, 54–8, 60, 61–4

Gabii, 28–30, 33
Gauls, 4, 56, 59–72, 79–82
Geryones, 9

Hamilco, 103
Hannibal, 4, 82 ff.
Hasdrubal, 98, 109–113
Hercules, 9–10
Herminius, T., 34
Hippocrates, 100, 103
Horace, 2
Horatii, 16–19
Horatius Cocles, 34–5, 37
Horatius Hostilius, 14

Juno, 55–6

Laelius, 98
Larcius, Sp., 34
Larentia, 7
Lars Porsenna, *see* Porsenna
Lentulus, L., 77
Livius, 109–10
Livy, 2–5

Luceria, 73-4
Lucretia, 30-2
Lysimachus, 117

Macedon, 113, 117-18
Maecius, 70
Maelius, Sp., 48-50
Manlius, son of M. Torquatus, 69-70
Manlius, L., 66
Manlius, M. Torquatus, 60, 63-5
Marcus Claudius, 46-7
Marcellus, M., 100-4
Marcius, Gn. Coriolanus, 4, 38-41
Mars, 7
Masinissa, 98, 100
Metaurus, river, 100-4
Mettius Curtius, 14-15
Mettius Fufetius, 16, 19-20
Middle East, 1, 113
Minucius, L., 48-50, 92-4
Minucius, 92-4
Mucius, C., 35-7

New Carthage, 106, 107
North Africa, 1, 82
Numidia, 98
Numitor, 6-8

Onomastus, 117
Ovid, 2

Padua, 2, 3
Palatine Hill, 5, 8, 9, 11
Papirius, M., 60
Perseus, 113-17
Philip the Fifth, 113, 117-19
Pompey, 1
Pontius, 73, 77-9
Porsenna, Lars, 34-8
Proca, 6
Prusia, 119

Quinctius Flamininus, T., 117, 119
Quinctius Poenus, 66
Quirinal Hill, 60

Racilla, 44
Remus, 5, 6-8
Rhea, 6-7
Romulus, 2, 4, 5, 6-8, 9, 11-16

Sabines, 11-16, 21
Sabine Women, 11 ff.
Saguntum, 82
Samnites, 69, 72-82
Scipio, 94-100, 104-8, 113, 119
Servilius, C. Ahala, 49-50
Servius Tullius, 22, 25-6
Sophonisba, 98-100
Sucro, 105, 107
Sulla, 1
Syphax, 98
Syracuse, 100-4

Tanaquil, 22-7
Tarpeia, 12
Tarquin the Old, 22-5
Tarquin the Proud, 25-34
Tarquinius, Sextus, 28-33
Tarquitius, L., 44
Tatius, T., 12-14
Thalassius, 12
Tiber, river, 7, 8, 9, 21, 34, 41, 43, 60
Trasimene, Lake, 89-91
Tullia, 25-7
Tullus Hostilius, 16, 19-20
Tusculum, 70

Valerius, M., 66-9
Valerius, P., 32
Varro, 92
Veii, 4, 21, 41-3, 51-7
Vergil, 2
Verginia, 46-8
Verginius, L., 46-8
Vestal Virgin, 7
Veturia, 40
Volsci, 38
Volscians, 40-1
Volumnia, 40